A Visual Approach to Park Design

A Visual Approach to Park Design

Albert J. Rutledge

Professor of Landscape Architecture
Iowa State University

Illustrations by
Donald J. Molnar

GARLAND

Library of Congress Cataloging in Publication Data

Rutledge, Albert J
  A Visual Approach to Park Design
  Bibliography: p.
  Includes index.
    1. Parks—Design and construction. 2. Parks—
Psychological aspects. 3. Environmental psychology.
I. Title. II. Title: Visual approach to park design.
SB481.R87   712′.2   80-28185
ISBN 0-8240-7258-8

Published by Garland STPM Press
136 Madison Avenue, New York, New York 10016

Printed in the United States of America

15 14 13 12 11 10 9 8 7 6 5 4 3 2 1

*With appreciation to
Anita, Dana, Elaine,
Ken, Larry, Lynn, Mary,
Pat, Ruey, Sue, and Zara*

Contents

Contents

SECTION THREE   **A People-Watching Prescription**

Introduction

"Surely we cannot
make good use of the
earth unless we have
some notion as to what
is good and what is
useful, what is aimless
change and what is goal
directed transformation."

Lewis Mumford

In my book *Anatomy of a Park*, I entitled a brief section, "Design Must Be for people," in which I suggested that "consideration of human habits as they might be accommodated in design is not presently common practice." This book is an elaboration upon that section. It is about human behavior—not everything you always wanted to know (because much remains a mystery), but perhaps a few things you were afraid to ask—for it will affirm that human habits are still too frequently ignored in park planning. It's about time for a concerted effort to correct that slighting. We'll suggest one way how.

This book is also about "good" as that term is used in evaluating environmental design.

It is commonly written that environmental designers strive to enhance our physical surroundings in the broad categories of function and aesthetics. You might, therefore, expect little argument that a "good" design is one that works as well as it is attractive. Countless examples measure up that way in practice. Obviously, many fall short of that mark as well. Some shortcomings can be attributed to the customary burdens of life: insufficient budgets or simply the mar-

1

ginal talents of perpetrators. Failures may also be traced to a dichotomy that afflicts environmental design at its core. Feeding an impulse to be eccentric, or perhaps covering up an inability to deal with one of the categories well, some practitioners have opted to reject either function or aesthetics and give exclusive attention to the other. Not too long ago, a national news magazine asked well-known designers to describe the task of their profession. One luminary declared that the job was "to create beautiful environments, that's all." He was slammed by an opposite who proclaimed that the "form doesn't count. What counts is whether or not the product functions."

Eccentricity may make good press. But it doesn't necessarily forecast good design. One camp asks us happily to accept roofs that leak or traffic that snarls as long as a spine-tingling aesthetic is present. The other would have us warm up to sound roofs and smooth traffic ways that look crummy. Such thinking smacks of the worst kind of professional elitism. It short-changes users, managers, and others who must live with the outcome once the designer removes himself from the scene. Evidence is ample that function and aesthetics are not mutually exclusive criteria. For those who have to live with the outcome, they are equivalently good.

Enough of that—for the moment at least. The contention has been raised here to show something about contentions per se. Regardless of what is frequently written, contentions are the usual order when it comes to presuppositions about what constitutes good planning practice, even at design's most general and time-honored level. Quarrels of every stripe abound. Some are deeply thought-provoking, as, for instance, the issue of human dominance over nature versus subservience to it. A number are pretty silly, at best lightly rooted in fashion, yet espoused no less intransigently: a belief in the cosmic virtue of curved lines versus movements which promote the transcendental value of angled forms. Yes, wars within the ranks of designers have been fought over such stuff. Profound or simple-minded, no matter, these arguments cannot be discharged as mere academic fancies. Design products are cast to reflect whatever version of good their producers have come to embrace.

This book joins the fray by adding *human behavior* to the argument over design criteria, not as a tangential matter, nor as a fashionable kick, but as a central concern. This book submits that environmental designs must service the behavioral needs of their users before they may be considered good. And it proposes to tilt the design process toward a search for form solutions that meet behavioral demands.

The assumption that professions exist to perform a service for others is contentious before it gets out of the chute. It runs counter to the viewpoint of those who refuse the service role, assume commissions as vehicles for artistic expressions of self, and oblige users to somehow make do with the results. Contrary to that viewpoint it shall remain. The call for a firm place for behavioral criteria may unsettle less obsessed designers who feel it could diminish attention to traditional concerns. Here rest at ease. While it asks for a reappraisal of popular criteria, nothing traditionally valued is meant to be cancelled out. Considering behavior is offered as another equivalent good.

While this book is inexorably tied to the stand that *good* design should continue to be defined as that which has high functional and aesthetic merit, it proceeds, however, from the recognition that there are usually innumerable schemes capable of meeting those standards for any given case. And it arrives at the posture that, in many instances, the *best* design will be the alternative most eminently sensitive to behavioral needs. Conventional artistic and technological creativity are scarcely meant to be suppressed. Just challenged a wee bit more.

Why should environmental designers embrace a dictum that so obstinately orders behavioral factors into their work? For openers, suffice it to say that every design impinges upon human behavior. On sheer weight alone, those decisions deserve to be made intelligently. The answer is as simple as that.

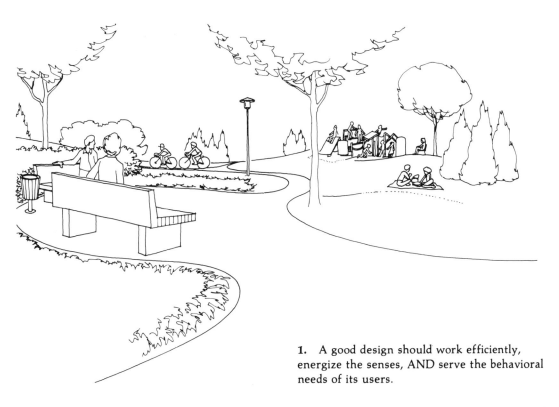

1. A good design should work efficiently, energize the senses, AND serve the behavioral needs of its users.

Regard how impingements upon behavior are implicit in every use label on a plan. To letter "Children's Play Area" on a spot, for instance, is to make a simple assignment. Yet it is a most presumptuous act. First, it implies that the users will be children, second, that they will "play" in that space and, moreover, that they will behave in a fashion consistent with the structures designed therein. Look elsewhere. Let's say that an item of sculpture has been sited and a setting designed to show it off. Perhaps the site has been developed to manipulate contemplative behavior through viewing channels and approach sequencing and benches where it is imagined that elderly people might choose to sit and admire the sculpture. Once more, and throughout, the designer has saddled the plan with expectations that certain populations will behave in particular manners in specific places.

The design is built. The people come in. Hello. Do the children snub the play structures and end up fooling around the benches and digging under the setting's ornamental plant display? Do teens take over the sculpture, drape themselves about like army ants, scale its heights, and adorn it with school numerals, first tentatively in chalk and eventually with spray paint, probably Day-Glo red? And do knots of old men grumble on the street corner at the sight of the youngsters' preoccupations, then retreat to a bar, however much they could have benefited from the sun and air?

It is not unusual to find analogous cases where the answer is yes, mishmashes of nonuse, misuse, and dissatisfactions, all traced to behaviors at odds with the plan. It has been argued that these kinds of problems rest with the user, that people do as they choose. But how many of these problems can be foreseen? For while behaviors are clearly manifestations of choice, many can indeed be anticipated and expected to occur with some regularity and can be dealt with in physical design. If designers

2. A plan is a statement of expectations about how a place will be used.

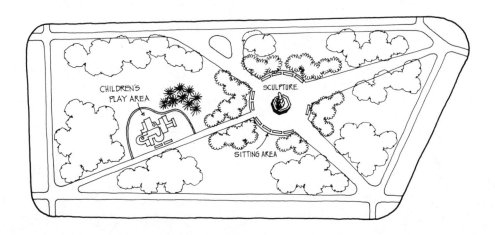

anticipate how people are apt to behave, they are likely to prevent problems that arise when expectations about a plan conflict with reality. When designers bungle or ignore planning for behavior, responsibility must be ascribed not only to users but to designers as well.

Putting an Eye on Behavior

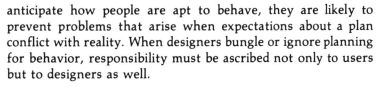

Knowledge about human behavior resides in the behavioral sciences. Ideally, then, designers may be seen as consumers of the scientists' efforts, the latter, in turn, responding to designers' calls for information needed in the course of their work. But it is only in the last decade or so that a dialogue has been attempted between these professions, and, with but a few exceptions, such an ideal is far from an operational fact. More typically, when a design practitioner and a behavioral scientist meet, an Alphonse and Gaston vaudeville routine goes into effect. The designer asks the scientist for design-relevant information; the scientist responds by asking him what he wants to know. They repeat themselves once more and then again, to the point that both end up stumped about even what questions to ask.

There is an ordinary impatience with this sort of thing which results in the designer lying in wait for the scientist to act. As a former president of the American Society of Landscape Architects stated neatly, his profession would "respond more to social and human needs as the social sciences afford better understanding of them." Among designers, therefore, it is popular to ascribe a lack of behaviorally based criteria to the uncertain state of behavioral science. As evidence, witness the inability of scientists to give designers direction.

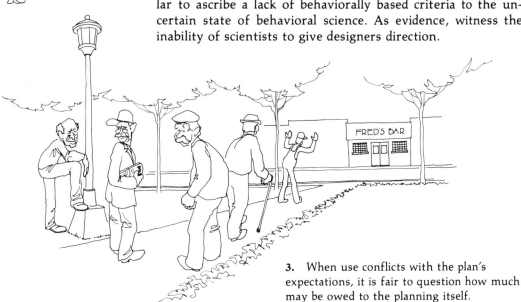

3. When use conflicts with the plan's expectations, it is fair to question how much may be owed to the planning itself.

4. This book suggests how the popular sport of people watching can become a design tool.

Nobody can deny that the field of behavioral science is inexact, characterized by more controversy than agreement, and not just when it comes to the relatively recent study of environment-behavior interaction. Even the venerable branches of science are fraught with contradictory theories, each with arguments compelling enough to confuse consumers about which is the most credible.

This book takes the stance, however, that a solution is available if designers would only exercise an initiative and look for it—literally *look* for it by watching behavior itself. In a sense, it is something that we all do already. Eat your hearts out, Bowie Kuhn and Pete Rozelle. *People watching* is the number-one national sport. Given proper focus, it can be a design tool. We already know that it can also be a lot of fun.

Section One of this book will demonstrate how people watching can produce a host of design-relevant insights, especially about how people use space. It will describe a number of findings by people watchers in the past and exemplify how they translate into design criteria.

Section Two will concentrate on why people use space as they do by highlighting some behavioral theories that not only appear relevant to design applications, but are at such a level of development as to be usable now as a foundation in which to root design decisions. The theory base will also provide a focus for the people-watching process itself.

Section Three will expand upon that focus by describing the kinds of information that the design-conscious people watcher ought to seek. This section is meant to show designers how to take advantage of the fortuitous interactions between people and environment which they might see as they walk down the street. It could also be used as a point of departure for systematic office procedures or rigorous research, including case investigations conducted by designers or behavioral scientists, if need be acting alone, or, more happily, in consort with each other. Section Three will also discuss a model for restructuring the design process so as to admit behaviorally based criteria on a sustaining basis.

This book concentrates on park planning applications. Yet it draws many of its examples from other areas of environmental design. This approach reflects the fact that, in the planning of physical places, there are a myriad of common concerns. Insights generated by the study of one project type are potentially transferable to others. For instance, general criteria for measuring design success or comments on the design process itself are clearly generalizable. Thoughts on behavioral theories as they affect park issues may have comparable impact on, say, housing matters. Conversely, housing analyses may produce parallel lessons for the planning of parks. Thus, while this book is primarily directed to park designers and administrators, its material is also useful for other environmental planning and management professionals.

Design and administrative practitioners may take this book as a prospectus for action. Students and professors may use it to formulate problem-solving strategies and field exercises. A basis for the latter are a number of drills called "Eyeball Calisthenics," which will be found liberally scattered about.

Behavioral scientists may also find this book of interest, if for no other reason than that they want more clearly to understand the design context into which some of their work might wend its way. Some may cringe at reading the simplified versions of complicated theories and at the promotion of reliance upon mere notions. But regard that the solutions to many problems actually lie in simplification, and to disdain notions is to avoid getting started. We cannot afford to wait for definitive answers when thousands of design decisions are being made daily without *any* allusion to behavioral thought.

As may be apparent, this book will not shrink from cantankerousness on occasion. To avoid needless argument, something should be said about what its posture does *not* imply. To urge the assembling of behavioral insights upon designers and to offer people watching as a productive means is not to cast designers as amateur behavioral scientists. Nor, in any other way, is it meant to usurp the prerogatives of those distinguished professions. Rather, it is to promote an attack on a topic from many directions. In the early stages of inquiry, every bit of information, however crudely assembled or incomplete, is productively revealing. Both designer and scientist have a stake in the outcome, and both have a perspective to furnish. Furthermore, by encouraging an active role for designers in marshalling behavioral information, the book should advance collaboration between the disciplines. People watching is a natural vehicle through which designers can most effectively participate. By training, they are visually oriented. To do what is asked herein is only to redirect a performance for which they are already uniquely prepared.

But be aware that while "a consideration of human habits as they might be accommodated in design" may seem like an agreeable intention and people watching may have a seductive ring, both will first call upon designers to adjust some attitudes, many of which go to the heart of park design as it has always been practiced. Moreover, unlike *Anatomy of a Park*, which deals with time-tested principles, this undertaking is charged with speculations. It is, therefore, not meant for the cautious, but addressed to those energized by the prospect of discovery and the will to experiment. Determination is also required, for experiments do not always run smoothly. The first wagon probably had square wheels, and it is easy to imagine the jostles that came with the ride. But the people who did jump aboard got to their destination a good deal faster than those who stood aside unwilling to take the risk.

Section One

People Watching in Your Spare Time for Fun and Profit

"People confer use on parks and make them successes or else withhold use and doom parks to rejection or failure."

Jane Jacobs

1 | The Elusive Reality Factor

On a midwestern college campus, there is a Hyde Park-style "free-speech" area developed at considerable expense in response to the persuasions of the 1960's. It is a handsome design, complete with precast concrete podium, brick pavement, benches, and backdrop plantings. Yet from day one, it has never witnessed a single invocation. Never lacking for causes, the speechmakers remain aplenty. But they deliver their pitches somewhere else. What attracts them to that other location and not to the one designed specifically to accommodate their needs? It is unlikely that the practitioner who created the custom setting will ever know. Indeed, the designer may not even be aware that the condition exists, despite the ease with which you might note the phenomenon. Both locations lie within sight of each other.

That designer is not alone. Few know the degree to which their projects are used, much less if the use is contrary to what the facilities were designed to support. Most call the job done upon the end of construction and seldom investigate what happens after use settles in. Beliefs about their work stay, therefore, largely untested. They are denied evidence of possible

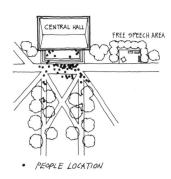

1.1 Note where the people are gathered.

THE CAMPUS FREE SPEECH AREA

1.2 Why does the speech-making take place in the unplanned area, while the spot designed for that purpose remains ignored?

misjudgments and left unguarded against the replication of similar errors in the next job around. They are also denied evidence of sound judgments and only luck governs whether belief and reality will mesh.

The Designer Is Predictor

No design budget that I am aware of has a line to fund a thorough look after construction, and it is common to blame the lack of use evaluation on that. I would submit that the source of prohibition lies much deeper. It involves fundamental matters of a designer's disposition which render even informal, uncomplicated and convenient looks at reality a low priority in many designers' minds.

Foremost is a reluctance to admit to a responsibility for how a designed place is peopled, ignored, or allegedly mistreated. A responsibility not to the absurd extent of assuming a legal or moral obligation for the acts of others, but in the following sense: a plan is a reflection of expected use. Yet plans do not think nor expect a single thing. Planners do, and their schemes reflect *their* expectations. Indeed, they mirror a planner's *predictions* about how a place will be used. Such predictions prove true when the physical forms and spaces that were proposed support well the behaviors that ensue. Conversely, when the designed environment and user behavior conflict, predictions have failed. That is at the heart of what this book would have you accept: the role of predictor comes with the territory. And any predictor worth his crystal ball is at least curious about how it all came out.

That is not a novel idea. Nor is the concept that every design project should have a follow-up analysis once the people come in. Yet because both remain short of routine application in conventional practice, we mention them here. We'll explore the matter of routine application in a bit of detail in Chapter 8. Now let's examine the more usual expectations at the beginning of the design process where the "predictions" are formed.

Priming Intuition

At the onset, an enviornmental designer assembles a program of activities which is believed appropriate to the site and which then gets translated into germane facilities. Subsequently, the facilities are organized on a plan to reflect his expectations. At the beginning, the question is, *How founded do those expectations happen to be?*

In the past, park planners placed much reliance upon popular conventions. Some conventions were like sets of national standards that generalized the kinds of activity areas that various types of parks should contain, regardless of who used them. Otherwise, trust was put in the designer's intuition, sometimes described as a mystical sense of correctness with which professionals are endowed.

Beginning a decade or two ago, national standards fell into question when people realized both that they stuffed parks into singular molds and that because different parks have different users, the emphasis should be on tailoring each site to the unique leisure needs of the subject population. These realizations fostered the execution of public surveys to assess recreational preferences and later, especially on the neighborhood level, direct involvement of residents in deciding how their parks ought to be planned.

During this shift, many designers also began to doubt the viability of their cherished intuition as a source for decision making. Perhaps victimized by the cry of the 1960's that consigned everything of the past to perdition, or taken by the notion that the placement of blind trust in survey data would elevate their art to that of an exact science, some turned their backs on intuition altogether.

The intuitive route is not without examples of abuse. Many designers hide behind it to avoid having to justify their moves. And some spin out of it such a mystique for themselves that they actually come to believe the Salvador Dali put-on that creative wisdom flows exclusively out of the end of one's moustache. But to disdain intuition is like shaving off your moustache, or more pointedly, lopping off your arm because occasionally it engages in a capricious act. Your future performance is bound

to suffer. While the generation of surveys and other means for public expression is a turn for the better, they produce but raw, sometimes conflicting, and usually incomplete information. Few people can articulate their every need, and ever present is the possibility of discrepancies between what people say and what they will actually do. Interpretations and augmentations are always needed. Quite often designers have no other resource but their instincts to arrive at sensible decisions. If still trusted, a designer's intuition merits enhancement. If mistrusted, it deserves to be reassessed.

While some would seem to have been graced with an intuitive mastery at birth, for most of us it is a hard-to-come-by facility which must be constantly nurtured. Enter *people watching* as a means to that end. It is available to anyone. For purposes of informing intuition, it demands no fancy instruments, no production-like arrangements, and, above all, no expense. Just a well-tuned eye. Watch people in the parks, to be sure, for that is the subject of this writing. But also people watch upon all occasions: while on your lunch break, cruising home from the office, in your rocking chair with julep in hand or wherever you happen to be. As subsequent examples will attest, insights gathered in just about any setting may have implications for park design.

Using casual means and exploiting happenstance, the ultimate aim is to paste bits and pieces into a mental encyclopedia on how people act in given situations. On the one hand, it is an expedient maneuver to build up a ready resource for instances when a grand study cannot be mounted. But it can also serve as a forerunner to the preparation and analysis of systematic research if conditions permit an extensive probe in conjunction with a specific design. In either case, the return from leafing through the pages of the mental encyclopedia should make the design process less of a crapshoot, and at least weight the odds on the side of predictive success.

Try it out. A people-watching habit is not unlike the routine of a congressman who returns periodically to his district to get reacquainted with his constituents lest he fall out of touch.

1.3 Make people watching a habit wherever you happen to be.

2 | How Do People Use Parks?

As a warm-up, simply watch what the people are doing. In a particular park you may see basketballers shooting hoops or maybe softball teams deployed. Sports like these are all structured events which ordinarily dominate a designer's program and therefore receive priority attention in the planning. Fine tune your observations and you may also see people standing, strolling, running around, sitting, lying, talking, playing a guitar, reading a paper, catching rays, walking a dog, teaching a youngster the fine art of frisbee throwing, enjoying a pipe—the list can go on ad infinitum. While each item taken alone may not seem of earth-shaking regard, a summary reflection could show that, over the course of a day, and quite possibly at any given time, *most of the people may be engaged in such outwardly incidental pursuits* as opposed to structured sports.

To See and Be Seen

The next thing you might discover when you people watch is that a healthy share are watching you back. Moreover, as landscape architect John Lyle reported from his study of Los Angeles

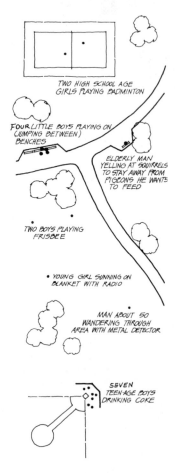

TWO HIGH SCHOOL AGE
GIRLS PLAYING BADMINTON

FOUR LITTLE BOYS PLAYING ON
(JUMPING BETWEEN)
BENCHES

ELDERLY MAN
YELLING AT SQUIRRELS
TO STAY AWAY FROM
PIGEONS HE WANTS
TO FEED

TWO BOYS PLAYING
FRISBEE

YOUNG GIRL SUNNING ON
BLANKET WITH RADIO

MAN ABOUT 50
WANDERING THROUGH
AREA WITH METAL DETECTOR

SEVEN
TEEN-AGE BOYS
DRINKING COKE

• PEOPLE LOCATION

2.1 Note how often the number of people engaged in seemingly incidental activities outweighs those involved in structured events.

parks, most will have chosen to lounge facing the direction of human activity, be that structured gaming, informal frolicking, or just plain passing by.

Lyle's study reminds us that people like to watch other people, and not just in Los Angeles. In a midwestern neighborhood park my associates and I studied, sunbathing was the most popular activity, or so it appeared upon an initial glance. Yet with many sunny locations to choose from, the vast majority selected to distribute themselves along the brow of a rise that afforded a clear view of "activists": frisbee and football throwers, hand-springing exhibitionists, others horsing around as well as basketball and tennis players in their respective courts on the opposite edge of the space. During follow-up visits (over the course of two years), we watched the sunbathers closely. Occasionally, some read or talked or listened to radios, but most spent their basking moments scanning the action over which their location had command.

Then there were those who enjoyed being watched in return. The feats of prowess displayed by the activists, for instance, were not especially noteworthy when few onlookers were present. But they grew bordering on exaggeration when a large audience was amassed. Similarly animated were sunbathers who settled adjacent to a well-traveled path; they sat up more frequently than function required to fiddle with their straps, snap the elastic on their Speedos, and lay on the oil. Most obvious was a muscular regular who, as a matter of clockwork, would perambulate along the path to a drinking fountain, all along twitching his biceps in the manner of a high jumper loosening himself for a run at the bar. Upon reaching his destination, he'd duck his head over the spigot, then return to his blanket for a respectable period before the next promenade. It wasn't thirst that prompted the routine—the drinking fountain was broken.

What's the Reason? Don't just rely on the say so of these couple of cases. Check it out for yourself, and there will follow the safe assumption that a significant amount of leisure time is tied up in seeing and being seen. The root of this phenomenon is possibly explained by planner Seymour Gold, who points to the studies of sociologist Herbert Gans that reveal how much recreation "tends toward involvement of the person in vicarious role playing and various sorts of fantasy that result in a different orientation toward the self." Whether the activity be watching Sunday afternoon football on the tube, the opera at the Met, or simply a lovely shadow in the night, delight comes from imagining oneself as the star in question or performing a skillful role in the scene. Or if one actually happens to be a

2.2 Note how often the people you watch are watching others.

halfback, contralto, or body beautiful at the center of attention, pleasure stems from building up a desired image of worth by perceiving the acknowledgment of others. But you know all about that. I dare say you've done so yourself.

Cultural analyst Amos Rapoport has spoken about how tendencies to fantasize about oneself are classically evidenced in the popularity of the detached, single-family dwelling. Its front is extensively exposed and can be adorned at will to project whatever self-serving image is desired. That image may be projected through the selection of landscaping style, color of house paint, what is displayed through the picture window, or (shudder) the hanging of moose horns over the garage door. At the same time, the impermeability of the wall and the distance from neighboring facades check activity from leaking out which might contradict the preferred image. Less controllable is the apartment unit. Exterior exposures are not only minimal, but their personalizing is usually discouraged. Moreover, incidents by which most of us would not care to be characterized, incidents like kicking the cat, squabbling with the family, to mention a few common occurrences, are audibly bared to whomever is on the other side of the shared thin walls.

It seems that the house as a controlled projection of self has moved into the park via the recreation vehicle. Observe any campground. The R.V. is more than a shelter on wheels. It too has become an object for image display. And, of course, most have citizens band radios and each operator a "handle" like Bronco Rider or Bodacious Mama. The use of handles is to present a picture of self under the best of conditions because over the airways what that handle conveys is about all that listeners have to measure you by.

Sometimes a Must. While it should not be astonishing to note that some pleasures are enhanced by access to an audience, more veiled is the fact that there are instances in which the eyes of others are essential if there is to be any pleasure at all.

2.3 Like the single-family house, the camper has become a vehicle for identity expression.

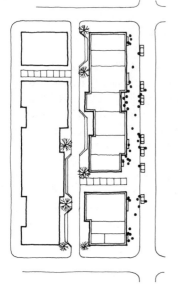

THE URBAN STREETSCAPE

• *PEOPLE LOCATION*

2.4 In many urban settings, the center of social interaction is along the fronts of the dwellings, not along the rear.

Consider the inner-city setting where an environmental designer after observing that car washing was a popular activity pledged to accommodate it in his neighborhood rehabilitation plan. In what he believed to be an enlightened upgrading of little-used land, as well as a means for eliminating congestion on the streets where he had witnessed the car washing, he proposed drainable surfaces, pipe stands, and amenities in the back alleys which were strung throughout the place. Hello again. Construction was completed and the ribbon cut. But the alleys remained devoid of cars while the car washing continued curbside on the streets.

What the designer ignored was the natural gathering of people along the fronts of the neighborhood buildings: adults clustered on stoops and leaning out of windows exchanging gossip, kids jumping rope on the sidewalk, men grouped around vegetable crates playing cards and, on hot summer evenings, hauling out a television set to watch the game. In this neighborhood, the front was the traditional center of social interaction. The back was where you piled the trash and, more than likely, where you went if you wanted to be mugged.

Albeit with good intentions of herding cars away as his contribution to tidying up the streetscape, the designer has suggested (predicted?) through his design that they be maintained where few eyes linger. It was to misunderstand that the incessant car washing was not as much of a janitorial pursuit (no car is so dirty as to warrant that much attention) as it was a pretext for the owner to associate himself with his car. Not unlike the R.V. with others in a crowded campground or the yacht anchored dockside in a jam-packed harbor, here the auto is a symbol of having made it somewhere along the line. To show off your wheels, though, you need an audience. But you can't just stand next to the thing for hours on end. So you

2.5 In places where people are watching, some people come out to be watched in return.

legitimize your presence by washing and buffing and tinkering under the hood, and you bask in the vibes that are coming from nearby idlers. And for at least those few moments, you're feelin' really good!

For the most part, in design as well as professional recreation circles, such activities as car washing and idling are treated as insignificant if not totally invalid uses of leisure time. Idling about is especially scorned. It is commonly defined as doing nothing; hence it is perceived as needing nothing special in the planning. Or worse yet, it is imagined as "the Devil's work," something to be summarily opposed. Let us leave the Devil's work notion for those taken by it to explain. Here a fresh assessment of idling seems necessary, for it is threaded throughout most of those outwardly incidental pursuits offered earlier as taking up vast amounts of leisure time. On the surface, idlers may appear to be doing nothing. But a closer inspection will show that a goodly number are—you guessed it—recreationally watching others and sometimes counting upon others to watch them in return.

Show Time May Be Any Time

The pervasiveness of the see-and-be-seen phenomenon leads to the following perception of the recreation place: *The park is a theater and each activity area a potential stage.* If this is accepted as a

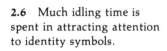

2.6 Much idling time is spent in attracting attention to identity symbols.

2.7 It's show time, folks.

planning axiom, it would raise some presently minor considerations higher up on the designer's priority scale.

Take the design attention usually given to sporting places, the most obvious stages with spectator appeal. Except for revenue-producing stadia or bleachers inserted during tournament times, designers incline their energies almost exclusively toward laying out fields, setting down courts, and otherwise favoring the routines of the actors. Little effort is extended to audience needs. This does not imply that all formal gaming areas should be surrounded by bleachers as if a World Series crowd were expected for every event. That is not only economically foolish, but I also suspect that their blatant presence would intimidate many players as well as potential onlookers and thus be counterproductive. Better to employ more subtle measures to enhance vantage points and the comfort of individuals and small knots of friends whose watching takes place in spurts.

That more subtle planning may involve no more than taking advantage of site potentials by tucking courts and fields below natural slopes or rock outcroppings, which then become inviting places for people to sit or lie with an elevated view. Or it may be simply a matter of orienting features serving other functions in the direction of activity, thus getting double duty from them. Adjust traffic-channeling earth mounds so that they face anticipated action; angle retaining walls toward the game as handy elements to sit upon or lean against; consider adjustments that afford views from far-off benches which may be closely associated with other use areas or dribbled about the park for respite. The latter, placing benches at distant vantage points, may be the most appreciated nuance of them all. In our midwestern park study, we were attracted by a young lady who

2.8 Orient idling accommodations toward the action.

sat away from the heart of the see-and-be-seen area across a creek that bisected the place. Yet, while well-separated from the action, much of her attention was given to a hot basketball game in progress on the opposite side of the channel. We were inclined to chalk it up as an inconsequential quirk in the pattern of things until advised by another woman that this was probably an introverted person who, while gaining pleasure from checking out the guys, was reticent in cueing others that such was the case. It was the reverse of the car-washing incident. Association was to be avoided. Anonymity was preferred.

Now, that's obviously a speculation which needs follow-up input (say, from the lady herself) before acceptance as an unalterable fact, and we'll speak to such needs at the beginning of Chapter 7. The Achilles' heel of observation is that it is clearly a speculative act. Yet, even when conducted absent of other measures, it can result in hypotheses of such probability that they deserve at least trial consideration in decision making. Better that then no trial at all. The hypothesis could turn out to be right. Consider, for instance, the potential in the charge we drew from this episode. *Treat distant viewing as consequentially as viewing from the edge of an action place.* Locations for the former may be called "safe spots." Their use can have physical implications as when the elderly who may derive pleasure from watching kids in the playground ought to be removed a bit so they won't be trampled by erratic play. But mostly safe spots serve to comfort the inhibited. And it matters not if the intimidating factors are more perceived than real, for, in the mind of the beholder, the impact is the same. Have you ever been a minority person in a public place? A straight in a gay bar? A Catholic in a Baptist church? A white transient workman in a black housing

2.9 "Safe spots" are places within view of the action, yet far enough away to comfort those who would be unsettled if they were in the midst of the scene.

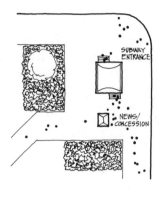

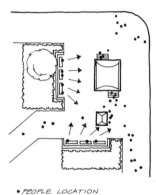

• *PEOPLE LOCATION*

2.10 Identify probable people concentrations and, as with the lower illustration, insert sitting facilities nearby.

courtyard? A canary reporter at a cat convention? Or simply new to a place? Were you nervous or comfortable? Was your action tentative or forward? Did you wade into the middle or hang back? Why? Would a seat in a "safe spot" have been to your liking, one from which you could also have surveyed the scene?

Anticipate Natural Congregating Spots.   Architect C. M. Deasy has observed that "of the various elements in a park that attract people, the strongest drawing card, ovewhelmingly, is other people." Thus to invite people to watch people by orienting resting accommodations toward the action is to advance overall interest in a place. Moreover, people watch people watching other people. To enlarge the audience is to increase the number of people to be watched. While that's rattling around, regard how routinely designers facilitate the viewing of other stuff, often with a great deal of precision: natural landscape scenes and man-made artifacts like sculpture, fountains, and impressive buildings. This book only urges that people concentrations be given equivalent due.

Structured sport areas are not the only potential stages in a park. In the thinking that precedes design commitment, pin down every probable congregating spot as a candidate for the treatments we've discussed. Consider major intersections, for example, or concession stands. Bring walking or bicycle paths serving routine traffic functions periodically within close view of anticipated people clusters. Provide rest stops there rather than in arbitrary locations about the site. Activity-intensive parks on the neighborhood, community, and city scale are obvious targets for such an approach as well as so-called "passive" urban malls, squares, and plazas. But there are also people pockets in large natural and historic interpretive parks—fee

2.11 Consider organizing entire use areas so as to enhance watching potentials from one to the other.

stations, refreshment stands, information plazas, tour marshaling areas—to which the notion may be extended, even though most of their acreage is put to low density inspection of non-human things.

Study the prospects of organizing entire use areas so as to maximize watching possibilities from one to the other. Locate complexes like picnic areas, for example, not simply so that they are convenient for foot access, for instance, to swimming pools, but so that they bring swimming and, especially, diving well into view. Weigh how the viewing between use areas might bring reciprocal gain. In an Illinois park, a playground was slotted between two banks of tennis courts for the mutual advantage of parents and preschool children who came in tow when such usual babysitters as teens and job-locked spouses were not on hand. This layout allowed adults to go about their sets and allowed the kids to go to the play structures, neither to stumble over each other, both remaining within comforting view. Many nontennis-playing parents benefited from this arrangement as well, positioning themselves near the playground so as to swivel easily between their kids and the nearby competitions. Indeed, many went to the extent of disdaining the playground benches, which focused only on the children's devices, to sit on those kids' play structures that had the best sight lines to the adult events.

Be alert to action just outside of the park on surrounding sidewalks, well-traveled streets, and such specific places as bus stops or where the popcorn man habitually parks his rig. Most parks turn their backs to their edges. In so doing, they may miss some of the most interesting people sights in town.

If for some reason you don't care to place extensive resting amenities where a people-watching enticement is great, you ought at least to prepare for potential idling of this sort. The

2.12 People watchers may lean or perch on handy facilities, whether you plan for it or not.

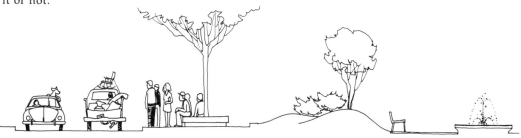

2.13 Design park edges to accommodate the watching of episodes just outside the site.

2.14 Consider setting idling accommodations away from entry channels.

users might do it anyway. Assume that fences will be mounted, lampposts leaned against, and planters perched in. Design them so that they are structurally capable of withstanding that impact, and don't plant fragile (not to mention botanically rare) species in beds that portend to be fifty-yard-line seats.

Of Course, Be Judicious. Although, as the car-washing example shows, there are cases in which watching ought to receive highest priority in the planning, there may be other occasions when lingering eyes are wholly obtrusive, and so no comfort, not even a planter for perching, should be extended their way. Efforts put to accommodating the viewing of public toilets and changing rooms are tacky, for instance. Designers should also be sensitive to places where crowds of watchers might pose a threat to passersby.

Entrances present a special problem. They may be prime watching spots, for, by definition, they will be traversed by many people. They may also be proximate to major street intersections whose cross traffic has potential viewing appeal. And they are logical places to wait for friends, a bus, or a pick-up car. Yet to outfit an entry with benches, leaning walls, and planters may clog it, not necessarily with physical obstacles, but with intimidating vibrations posed by the people who would sit in the place. This situation can be especially unnerving when the entering person has an acculturated suspicion, if not outright hostility, toward the gathered others and/or perceives them to hold a similar attitude toward him. It should be reemphasized that the presence of actual danger may be an irrelevant point, for perceiving danger can be an irrational act. Many elderly are automatically unsettled by the sight of teens milling about,

2.15 To flank entrances tightly with idling accommodations may set up an unnerving gauntlet for users to run.

conventional citizens discomforted when forced to make it through a throng of freaks, shoppers upset by derelicts draped in their path. Consider then the offsetting of idling accommodations well to the sides of an entry channel, particularly if it is the only apparent entrance when groups with built-in anxieties about each other are anticipated to make regular use of a place. If the animosities are severe, place the idling amenities a bit into the park yet still within view of the entry interest. That placement would apply the "safe spot" idea with reverse objectives as to who gets the relief. More on that when we speak about the design relevancy of behavioral theories in Chapter 6.

At the least, avoid wrapping high-use facilities around a sole park entrance. Otherwise, you might share the dilemma of officials in a central California city who were puzzled about why a tot lot placed in the short leg of an L-shaped park was receiving negligible use by mothers and children, even though they lived numerously about. See Fig. 2.16. The tot-lot location was seemingly ideal in that it was around the corner from a basketball court, thus isolated from the boisterous teens playing in the latter space. But the park entrance lay adjacent to the basketball court. Observations revealed not simply the occasional spillover of bodies from the court, but a chronic gathering of girlfriends and teen boy-watchers all over the entry walk. And, sure enough, interviews disclosed that the mothers were put off by the prospect of having to thread their way gingerly past the teenagers and forbade their kids to try it alone. So they all stayed home.

Jogging the Memory

That people like to watch other people is a well-known fact. It is also a foregone conclusion that people go to parks upon occasion to retreat from others or, at least, because they do not need a public association for the moment. In our midwestern park experience referred to a few pages ago, we also discovered such types: introspective singles, couples involved only with each other, small groups chatting in inward-facing circles. See Fig. 2.17. While the "see-and-be-seen" people went about their business in one discrete section, these "self-contained" subjects were mostly scattered about a tree-studded lawn in another section, across the creek, where we had also noticed the lady with the surreptitious eye on the distant basketball game.

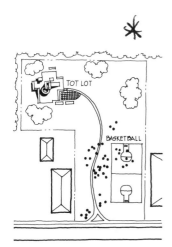

THE L-SHAPED PARK

• *PEOPLE LOCATION*

2.16 Mothers refused to navigate through the teen assembly, and so the tot lot went unused.

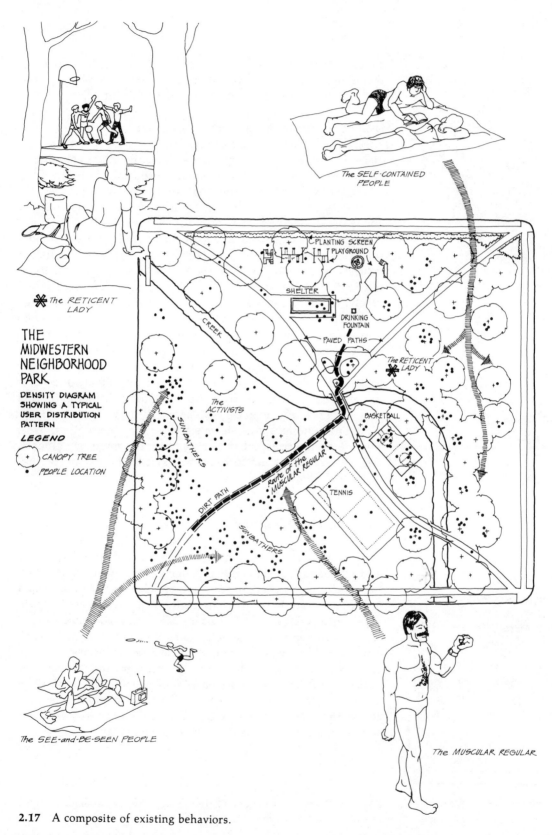

The SELF-CONTAINED PEOPLE

✳ The RETICENT LADY

THE MIDWESTERN NEIGHBORHOOD PARK

DENSITY DIAGRAM SHOWING A TYPICAL USER DISTRIBUTION PATTERN

LEGEND

✿ CANOPY TREE
• PEOPLE LOCATION

PLANTING SCREEN
PLAYGROUND
SHELTER
DRINKING FOUNTAIN
PAVED PATHS
CREEK
The ACTIVISTS
The RETICENT LADY
BASKETBALL
SUNBATHERS
Route of the MUSCULAR REGULAR
DIRT PATH
TENNIS
SUNBATHERS

The SEE-and-BE-SEEN PEOPLE

The MUSCULAR REGULAR

2.17 A composite of existing behaviors.

26

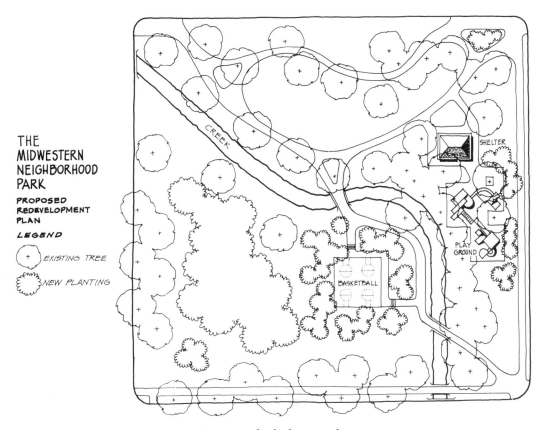

THE
MIDWESTERN
NEIGHBORHOOD
PARK
PROPOSED
REDEVELOPMENT
PLAN
LEGEND

(+) EXISTING TREE

NEW PLANTING

CREEK

SHELTER

PLAY
GROUND

BASKETBALL

2.18 A proposal which ignored existing routines.

Ironically, common facts may be so taken for granted that they are forgotten about in the planning. If observation serves one thing, it is to keep the memory alive. Witness the redesign plan (Fig. 2.18) proposed independently of our observations. Note its insensitivity toward what we saw taking place. Keep in mind that the neighborhood population is stable and that the present activities should be expected to remain a part of the use fabric for the foreseeable future.

The proposal suggests densely groved trees on the brow where the sunbathers now gather to continue around the edge of the creek. That grove would leave only a sun hole in the center, which is where the spontaneous players presently prance. The basketball courts would be sunken and hidden from all but immediate view. So much for sunbathers' vantage points and people-watching interest. A major playground investment has also been suggested, which is questionable in itself, considering that the present equipment is rarely used, in this case undoubtedly because few kids live near the park. More chilling is the scheduled transfer of the play area from its existing

27

wayside location to right smack in the middle of where the self-contained people find solace. What's left for them? Perhaps the vacated wayside? That is to jest, for the wayside is adjacent to a truck-belching avenue, and the fence which now separates them is to be torn down and the space rimmed with walks. Across the creek? Well, then, where is it anticipated that the gregarious sunbathers will be best served?

In short, what leads the designer to believe (as is surely his obligation) that his plan is a significant improvement and not just an expensive facility reshuffling that will leave the users no better off, if not lessen their enjoyment?

A Frame of Reference

One purpose of this section has been to introduce quickly a number of touchstones as references for the dialogue to come. Moreover, they are the cornerstones upon which this book is built.

1. There is the pivotal idea of design as prediction and designer as predictor. Through plan commitments, the designer prophesizes what will go on in the constructed work.
2. In that many predictions are grounded in conjecture, analyses of outcomes should become an integral part of the design process.
3. In order to advance the rate of predictive success, designers should be building up a mental encyclopedia of behavioral routines and their design implications by observing human events wherever they happen to be.
4. As for human behavior itself, we have touched upon the possibility that, in conjunction with overt activities, there may be hidden dimensions that deserve to be treated in design if user satisfaction is to be brought about.
5. We have also presented a chain of mental events which illustrate in an optimal manner how people watching can be made operational for design:
    a. We have *observed an overt activity* (sunbathing) and determined where it occurred in a particular place.
    b. We have *discerned something veiled about that activity* which seems normally wound up in the event (sunbathers were there to see and be seen).
    c. We have *tied that veiled dimension to a theory* (Gans's fantasy idea).
    d. We have *translated a readily observable phenomenon and its veiled dimension into a design criterion* not only relevant to a particular case, but also generalizable to other places where that phenomenon might occur. Furthermore, girded both by theory and its apparent association with a host of overt

activities, we have expanded that generalization to apply to park design at large (the park is a theater and each activity area a potential stage).

e. We have *developed a number of ways in which the criterion might be satisfied* (orientation of places toward the action, etc.).

Section Two will delve into the fundamental nature of human behavior as well as the professional behavior of designers themselves. It will embellish many of the above points and add a few more as to behaviors that may be considered for treatment in park design. Further light should, therefore, be cast upon what people watchers might be on the outlook for in their spare time for fun and profit. Don't wait though. Start looking now. If you wish, be guided by the "Eyeball Calisthenics" that begin nearby and appear periodically as this volume proceeds. They may be executed merely as warm-up exercises. Or, who knows, they may also generate a finding bearing back upon a design problem immediately at hand.

Eyeball Calisthenic 1

OBSERVE THE ACTIVITIES ON A SITE to become aware of a place's use and user complexity. Sit where as large an area as possible is visible without having to move. On the top of a pad (a lunch bag or envelope will do just as nicely), note the day, date, time, and weather conditions. Then, for a half hour or so, make a list of who is doing what. Give as much consideration to outwardly incidental pursuits as "four teenage boys drinking pop and talking" as you do to such planned activities as "a middle-aged woman jogging." Cite activities for each new arrival as well as major changes in behavior for those previously noted. At the end of the observation period:

1. Rank order the types of users according to how many times each appeared on your list.
2. Rank order the different activities also according to how many times each occurred.
3. To the best of your recollection, identify where the most "popular" user types were found and where the most "popular" activities took place.

PONDER: Can any of the activities be uniquely associated with any of the user types as if they might be expected to occur regularly with similar users in that time and place? Where did the most popular user groups locate; is there a discernible explanation for the selection? Where did the most popular activities occur; is there a discernible explanation?

29

REPEAT the exercise at the same time and place on another day. Then change times. Repeat the exercise in another, yet similar, place. What coincidences and differences occur? Why?

Eyeball Calisthenic 2

OBSERVE POPULAR PLACES to help forecast where people might naturally congregate. Either sit where most of the site is visible (as might be possible from an elevated level) or cruise about the place. Mentally, or on a piece of paper, note day, date, time, and weather conditions. Then, considering (but not limiting yourself to) the following characterizations, describe the places where knots of people happen to be:

1. *In relation to other people* (specify at busy intersections, near street musicians, where children are playing, etc.).
2. *In the near vicinity of functional units* (specify food-vending stands, advertising kiosks, etc.) *or significant physical features* (specify water displays, clock towers, etc.).
3. *In association with physical attributes* (specify elevation changes, bright colors, sharply delineated spaces, etc.).
4. *In connection with climatic factors* (specify sun, shade, etc.).

PONDER: Are there places where you believed you would find people or places devoid of people, yet discovered the opposite to be true; is there a discernible explanation?

REPEAT the exercise at the same time and place on another day. Then change times. Repeat the exercise in another, yet similar place. What coincidences and differences occur? Why?

As your experiences grow, begin to rank order places according to their see-and-be-seen potential, organizing them in four "probability" chunks:

1. Most likely regularly to attract substantial numbers of people.
2. May occasionally attract substantial numbers.
3. Seldom attracts substantial numbers, but may attract singles, couples or small groups engaged in self-contained pursuits.
4. Least likely to attract anyone.

Continue to "fine tune" the listing. Regroup places if further evidence warrants, but avoid major surgery upon witnessing occasional exceptions. Rather, if say, you come upon a "most likely place" that is vacant, first try to discern the cause. Cite that parenthetically as a condition for modifying the general rule.

Section Two

A Theory Foundation

"Knowing the answer
puts a different
perspective on the
question."

Nick Yamana

3 | Designers and Behavioral Scientists: Uneasy Bedmates

Interdependent as the ideal would have them, designers and behavioral scientists, nevertheless, grow up in different parts of town. (Some would say different countries.) Each has had to adapt to the idiosyncrasies of the other, and it has turned out to be a long learning task.

The disciplines are naturally set apart by the time frames in which they are used to conducting business. To the designer, time is always money. Each job is closed-ended, with a strict deadline for completion. In a public agency, overshooting the deadline pares down, if not eliminates, other projects. Funds must be borrowed from other projects to finish the lingering work. In private practice, missing the deadline raises the specter of no profit, and if repeated often, no practice at all. In design, "research" is almost exclusively case-specific. Frequently, it is conducted "quick and dirty," and therefore seldom arrives at conclusive answers. It is largely put to assembling whatever gross bits of background on the project are handy in the allotted time. If the budget is severely limited, research is the first step in the design process to go. Reliance for decision making reverts

3.1 Designers race the clock.

to experience, sufficient or not. Moreover, to some, skipping the research phase brings secret relief, for it allows them to get right to "designing," where their primordial appetites lie.

Mention research to a behavioral scientist, however, and typically it will be perceived as the pursuit of "truth," however long it might take. The scientist is as comfortable with the raising of questions as the securing of answers, if for no other reason than that the elicitation of a provocative question advances the likelihood of another grant appearing once the immediate funds run out. For some, it is as if the only deadline that counts is the far-off end of a personal career. At any rate, each job proceeds as an open-ended inquiry and is seldom addressed to a particular case, except insofar as casework may serve as a medium for inquiry. Scientific truth making demands precision. With time on their hands, behavioral scientists characteristically nudge notions along in increments and restrict their experiments to as few variables as possible. This tendency often produces "factlets" that may not have the same impact outside of the laboratory. In the realm where designers operate, the variables are hardly ever so stringently controlled.

Even when these fundamental obstacles of professional conditioning have been overcome, operational unsettlements still loom over joint ventures. Research issues which are relevant to the project (as opposed to merely what the researcher is curious about) must be identified, and the degree of research precision required must be mutually understood. Few projects can afford the behavioral scientist like the one who spent a year and miles of computer printouts for a 200-page report on circulation that said people get restive waiting for elevators. There must also be an implicit commitment to follow through on the results. Not many collaborations can maintain themselves if the designer ignores findings just because they run contrary to time-held conventions. To accomplish all that, both sides must talk. That alone is no mean task. Behavioral scientists incline towards seeing the world through statistical models and answering questions in quantitative terms. Designers read graphically and tend to think more about qualitative problems to which numbers may not relate. Furthermore, each discipline has its mysterious language. Designers are fond of dazzling others with such words as "infrastructure," for instance, whereas scientists like to tell us that "no mammal can structure a cognitive environment largely independent of its draco-limbic need to know conspecifics personally."

A means for smoothing the way to interdisciplinary collaboration is found in the idea of architect Raymond Studer and other early champions of behaviorally sensitive environments. Let design be perceived by scientists and designers alike as an experimental process. Indeed, as we will explore in Chapter 8,

3.2 Behavioral scientists search for truth.

the idea extends to treating design criteria as more than objectives to be met in a plan, to treating them as hypotheses, and to treating the project, once built, as a laboratory for testing out what amounts to a series of hunches.

The Theory Quest

To prepare for productive collaboration or parallel work, it would also do well for practitioners of each discipline to become familiar with the other in order to anticipate the directions from which the other might come. For the designer, this preparation can begin with an understanding of behavioral theories presently active in the scientist's realm. Upon trying that, some designers have stopped early on with their appetites killed, for the behavioral literature is fraught with contentions. Yes, like those suppositions about good design, testy postures are also the behavioralist's rule. In science little would seem to be fact, not even the fundamental matter of how behaviors are formed. Some scientists argue that behaviors are instinctive reflexes imprinted from birth; others of equal academic stature claim that, no, all behaviors are learned. One school would trace behaviors to attitudes; another reasons that attitudes defy definition, hence cannot be measured, and offers that behavior itself begets behavior, one person's actions triggering a response from another. Is it, then, as planner Constance Perin once suggested: "In spite of all the confusion, there seems to be one point of agreement—the situation is impossible"?

Confusing, yes. Impossible, no. Where contentions rage, it does not necessarily follow that one is as worthless as another. Rather, until refuted beyond question (the world should no longer be considered flat), one argument may be taken to be just as acceptable as the opposite. A person who needs to operate in such a Never Never Land can therefore embrace the notion with which he feels comfortable. The situation is akin to being confronted by an unfamiliar fork in the road. You can stand about and go nowhere, or you can select one of the paths off of a gut reaction and follow it until something along the way either bears out the wisdom of the selection or indicates a dead end. The best that behavioral theorists have to offer now is a map full of forks, and the history of behavioral science suggests that we must operate under the probability that this will always be the case.

In the sections that follow you will be exposed to a select number of theories that form an operational foundation for design. It is the foundation with which I feel comfortable; therefore, these sections present a most biased view. You may take umbrage at this approach, preferring to see the whole range of

35

arguments displayed, without editorial emphasis, for you to choose among. Fine. Choose what you like, as I'm sure you will, but you'll also have to provide your own reasoning. In any event, let my biases be challenges to your preconceptions. Received in that fashion, they may hopefully lead to a theory foundation that comforts you. But in embracing your own theories, remember that you ought to remain alert to evidence that can build up a personal conviction about their claims. Once more, people watching is a handy means.

The Bruise and Bounty of "Coming off the Wall"

Developing a theory foundation may seem like an awful lot of busy work. Why need theory at all? What's the return? Theories are plausible explanations about observed facts. They explain cause and effect and supply a comforting consistency to intervening acts. Curiously, though, we begin with the brazen pronouncement that agreement at the theoretical level is not essential to a designer's delivering a behaviorally sensitive design. For example, a few chapters hence I will ascribe some observable phenomena to territorial behavior. You may disagree that the behavior is territorial or disbelieve that humans have territorial tendencies or even reject territoriality as a credible theory from the start. But you must believe that what is being observed is occurring, and you can deal productively with that fact alone. As a friend of mine once said: "They first built bridges because there were crevasses to cross, and they were successful centuries before anyone came along with a theory about how bridges worked." Design is an experimental process. Without a theory in hand, it's just a riskier business.

"Coming off the wall," you might sorely miss the mark, as landscape architect Paul Friedberg freely admits happened to him when he describes his design for a New York City park. He took pains to provide the elderly "with a place of their own, carefully cloistered from the more boisterous people who would also be using the large plaza," only later to witness them scrupulously avoiding the place. The elderly population "wanted none of this seclusion and went out on the sidewalks again where they could be participants—however passively—in the drama of life."

You could also hit the mark squarely, even to the extent of starting the kind of creative revolution Friedberg accomplished with his facility designs for children's play. Note how a casual observation precipitated Friedberg's work. As he tells it, during an inspection of a site under construction, he saw children cavorting on boards, sawhorses, and other materials remnants, which they had connected to form a series of circuits. Their construction inspired him to link pieces together in the play-

3.3 After the workman retired, children were observed organizing construction materials into a series of circuits.

3.4 The construction-site episode inspired the linking of pieces in designed play environments.

ground for the New York City park, in contrast to the traditional manner of spotting apparatus about, one piece in isolation from another. Subsequently, the concept of *linkage* has been taken up by an untold number of playstructure designers.

Theory and Practice in Concert: Playground Design

While the linkage idea came to pass absent of a theoretical base, it is actually supported by a psychological theory that was being translated into a design-relevant condition by child psychologist Michael Ellis (then Director of the Children's Research Center at the University of Illinois) at the very same time that Friedberg was making his independent deductions a thousand miles away. As another irony, the traditional playground of isolated swings, climbers, see saws, etc., which linkage opposes, resulted from application of another psychological theory.

3.5 Linkage opposes the conventional procedure of spotting apparatus about.

3.6 The surplus-energy theory spawned the creation of unidimensional pieces which were meant to be played upon according to a fixed routine.

In days of yore, theorists supposed that children played to burn up surplus energy. "Play needs" were imagined as a number of motor exercises, and the playground was imagined as a place where children could go to slide, swing, climb, jump, and otherwise acceptably purge the ferment from their systems. The playground piece emerged as a unidimensional contrivance. It accommodated a single exercise. Furthermore, kids had little say in how each piece could be used. Not only was a slide just for sliding, they had to slide in a manner dictated by its design. The conventional playground thus became a scattered assortment of apparatus, each used according to a predetermined ritual.

Several who have observed use of these conventional playgrounds have discovered it to average on the order of fifteen minutes. Play time upon each piece was found to be fractionally less, sometimes only a number of seconds. I suppose that surplus-energy theorists would argue that the children only needed such brief encounters to expend the energy that bubbled within them. Equating quiescence on the part of the children with satisfaction, these theorists would take the findings on use patterns as a sign of the playground's success. But the data could just as well be taken as evidence of the youngsters' boredom with the playgrounds—hardly a basis for applause. Boredom is the likely case in light of a more recent theory called "optimal arousal," as described by Ellis in his book *Why People Play*.

Ellis shows how *play is an arousal-seeking behavior* and that *children play for the stimulation they receive*. It would seem then that children are not intrinsically motivated to play to burn up surplus energy. Nor do they seek out a play environment to become physically fit, socially skilled, conceptually aware or historically attuned, even if they achieve those objectives as by-products of play and even if those pursuits might appear advisable in the eyes of adults. Put simply: play is an end in itself. Call it fun.

Ellis offers the opposite of quiescence, "stimulation," as a sign of satisfaction. For a playground to be potentially stimulating, he maintains that it should be capable of eliciting continual responses from the children as they play and that these responses should "increase in complexity as play proceeds." The primary deficiency of traditional equipment is its absence of complexity, in one sense, its inability to offer possibilities of a higher order once its most obvious use ritual has been mastered. The same relative simplicity per piece casts degrees of suspicion upon a host of contemporary alternatives in playground equipment, whether they be retired fire trucks, ersatz rocket ships, cutesied-up cartoon or nursery rhyme structures, imitation Dodge City streetscapes, or artsy architectural sculptures. In other words, theoretically speaking, a lot of the stuff which is being purchased for playgrounds fails miserably in stimulating creative play. That judgment would also include many of the modular designs which appear to apply the Friedberg idea but do not go far enough.

Simplicity is out. *Complexity* is in. To make that term operational in design, Ellis advises that when faced with a choice of play pieces or layouts, select that which (1) allows the child to manipulate it in the greatest variety of ways, (2) allows for the most cooperation among children (kids seeming to play more spiritedly in the company of peers), and (3) inhibits the behavior of the child the least. The device or layout that scores out the highest is the most complex; it has the greatest stimulus potential; it can be said to possess the most "play value."

Adventure Play Graduates with Honors. The ultimate application of these guidelines thus far is the Adventure Playground. Originated and still going strong in Europe, this concept, which encourages children to construct, modify, tear down, and rebuild their own play environments out of scrap material, has slowly begun to be implemented in the United States. Proceeding through the three Ellis guidelines, we have the child operating constantly at his own capability level. Therefore the behavioral frustrations singled out in item 3 above may be practically nonexistent. Also, because the construction process inherently leads to calls for assistance, the group activity implied in item 2 is fairly well assured. Mostly though, it is in the first category of manipulability where the Adventure Playground scores highest. Even when something becomes erected, the parts remain manipulable, for nothing prevents them from

3.7 The optimal-arousal theory supports the Adventure Playground concept.

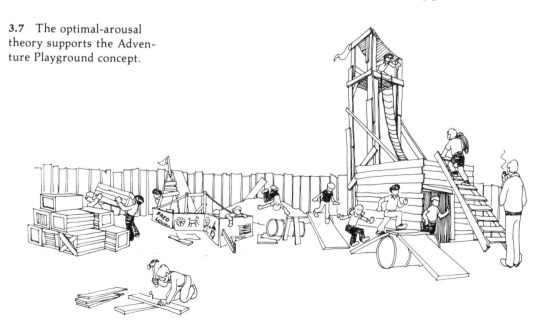

being changed around or the structure from being wholly dismantled. Indeed, such experts as my then eight-year-old son would have us believe that doing the latter is the most fun of all. As he mentioned once while on the beach: "The best part of building a sand castle is being able to kick it down."

Yet while all that potential is present, there is general agreement among recreation people that the actual effectiveness of an Adventure Playground is dependent upon the quality of the unobtrusive but readily available adult leadership which inspires the kids, answers their questions, ensures their safety, and arbitrates such passionate disputes as might occur should my eight-year-old kick down another kid's castle. Adult leadership is a critical conditioner. An Adventure Playground requires not only leadership but also controlled access and scheduled hours. What remains available for play when staff cannot be counted on, when the schedule doesn't coincide with children's desire to play, and when parks are of such limited size that the messy visuals are more than the neighbors and users can be expected to take? Most of the time, public parks are unsupervised and open for spontaneous use. Because of these problems, the majority of facilities must have a greater degree of structural soundness than the build-up–break-down Adventure Playgrounds.

If we refer to theory and the spinoff guidelines, the provision of structural soundness is not as terrible a sacrifice as some have argued. Manipulability, especially, can be provided by any number of well-built items that move with or against the child as he plays: cargo nets, swinging ropes, taut rubber sheets, bridges that undulate upon being crossed, tire swings that can be bounced independently or against a neighbor's, water features that surprisingly spurt from one aperture when a finger is held over another, etc. Many outwardly simple items can provide the most complex structures when put to use: moldable sand and fluid water, for instance, not to mention ingenious structures like one I once happened upon that was full of nothing but brightly colored, oversized ping pong balls. Reminiscent of a contained, backyard leaf pile, the structure was deliciously inviting to jump in, dive in, bob up and down in, wade drunkenly amidst, and it invited you to throw cascades of balls either in the air or lightly at your friends. Admittedly, the structure was in a supervised park and probably would not last long in an unsupervised place. But the thought is tempting. To make something manipulable, yet structurally sound, presents a challenge to designers' creativity. But that's why they earn big money.

Linked Systems Take Honors, Too. Another dimension of manipulability refers us back to linkage. To connect pieces is to turn the playground into a total system. Each piece not only retains its own play value, but also becomes a route to another.

Thereby, the *children can manipulate themselves* all around each piece, straight across, up and down, in and out, and in a great variety of ways. The best-linked systems even bring what is generally treated as merely functional elements into the act. Struts may be angled and notched for climbing, crosspieces broadened for scooting, wall members caused to rise and fall for giant-stepping, etc. A great deal of complexity can therefore be managed even where the most enduring materials must be employed. There is also an inspired role for traditional apparatus. Where a custom-designed, linked system is slated to replace an old nearby playground, it might be economically wise for the designer to scavenge the latter for its most worthy pieces and to incorporate

3.8 In a designed environment, manipulability may be provided by items that move with or against the child as he plays.

them in the new design either as termini to routes (as a slide could become) or bridging elements between units (as monkey bars might serve).

In a linked system, potentials for cooperative play are found notably in individual pieces which traditionally were designed to be used by one child at a time, but since have been enhanced to serve several. As opposed to single seat units, tire swings, for instance, can handle one, two, or three. In contrast to the restrictions posed by the conventional narrow chute, wide gang slides or several slides coming down side by side can be used by both singles and groups. The linking elements are also involved with swinging ropes positioned so that a buddy must fling the rope end up to a Tarzan or Jane before he or she can leap off. The children's inventiveness about uses takes care of the rest, as in the case of the kids who discovered that if one pounced full force on the end of an undulating bridge, a tsunami-sized wave would bounce everyone else on the span high in the air.

So as not to inhibit play behavior, a successful linked system offers gradations in difficulty. Thus it contains something for everyone within the age groups that playgrounds attract, no matter any child's capability level at a particular time.

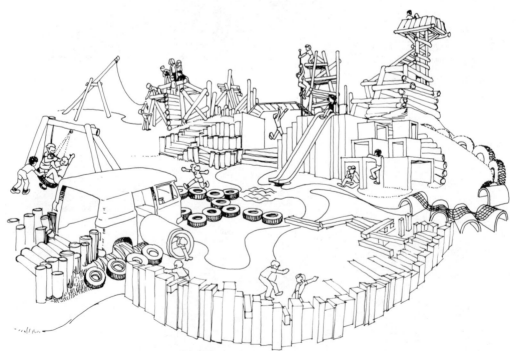

3.9 Linked systems offer circuits around which the child can manipulate himself in a variety of ways and also provide enclosures for more ordered activity. They also offer items which encourage cooperation and graduations in difficulty which correspond with a child's changing capability level.

3.10 In a linked system, alternative courses of action are available at key points.

Most important, in keeping with the Ellis dictum that complexity should increase as play proceeds, the same system also responds to a child as his capabilities change over time. It would therefore offer such structures as sliding poles to be addressed from varying heights, or bridges which can not only be traversed but also jumped on or dangled from or approached by ramp or by hopping from brace to brace or by pulling up a rope, with the rope concurrently available for swinging, etc. This arrangement flies in the face of the old standards that told us to have separate play structures for different age groups. There is no precise correlation between chronological age and development level. Except for providing alternative complexes for toddlers who have not reached a stage of alertness that will allow them to mingle safely with older children, designers should ignore separate age group thinking. A well-designed linked system is ever ready for the child and has another dimension for discovery once its simpler phases have been transcended.

Linkage also has its quantitative side. By incorporating the space between discrete structures into the play scheme, linked systems accommodate more kids than a scattering of unidimensional items taking up the same square footage. Furthermore, in that linkage increases the number of play possibilities for each structure, alternatives are available for dissipating occupancy wars should some youngsters monopolize any single feature.

Are linked systems safe? To my knowledge, no systematic data has been collected to answer that question. Conceivably, accidents could occur on them, for it is impossible to imagine a totally casualty-free environment for active youngsters. And that restriction includes traditional playgrounds where it is not unknown for kids to have run into the path of a careening swing seat. In a linked system, odds are that the cause of accidents will be traced to overzealous horsing around on the part of the kids or to isolated design defects like an exposed bolt end, ragged platform edges, or a plank stupidly made to jut into a movement path rather than to anything inherent in the concept itself. For the linkage idea has a safety feature not present in the ordinary equipment. Responding to a warning system apparently built into kids that deters them from fulfilling routines they don't think they can handle, linked systems provide optional escape routes. A traditional slide, for instance, ensures problems for the child who gets to the top and balks at the prospect of having to go down. He turns on a tiny, slick platform only to find other kids yapping at his heels and blocking his sole avenue of retreat. In a well-designed linked arrangement, the slide is only one way down from a broad, raised platform. The child can contemplate this arrangement from a distance and can go down when ready or take a less death-defying route, perhaps a ladder, sliding pole, ramp, or bridge. And he can do so without, I suspect, a loss of face among his peers and certainly without bringing his parents into a state of cardiac arrest, a common reaction in parents whose offspring stands petrified at the top of an ordinary slide.

Testimony from Observations. Considering my previous stance that one ought to build up a personal conviction about theoretical claims, I do not base this promotion of linkage merely upon trust in someone else's high-sounding words. My experiences and that of my associates bear out my contentions. For example, my colleague, landscape architect Robert Callecod, conducted a systematic investigation of scores of third graders at two playgrounds. Both sites were similar in size and number of structures. They differed in that one was a well-done linked arrangement and the other a disconnected assortment of traditional swings, slides, spring horses, roundabouts, etc. Callecod and his young subjects made many visits to both playgrounds over a number of weeks to minimize the influence of novelty. Each time, the same children were asked to express their preferences as to the entire site, individual elements and the manner of play allowed. Their replies were compared against time-lapse movie coverage of their play. Preference expressions and actual use coincided, sounding overwhelming favor for the linked complex.

What's the reason? Optimal arousal theory aside for the moment (but in the end reinforced), we have concluded from other observations that linkage accommodates a normal penchant of children to play in random patterns. By offering a host of circuits at varying levels, it does so in a highly versatile fashion. Because fate was being unusually kind one day, a foul-up in our methodology brought this conclusion to our attention. Attempting to determine which pieces in a traditional playground attracted the children the most, we were manually recording their locations at periodic intervals and looking up each time at a scene before transferring it to a map. The method

3.11 Watch children at play in natural settings to discover tendencies which call for support in designed environments.

sufficed when a handful of kids were present. When hordes were there, however, it not only became impossible to capture the scene in one glance, but with every successive glance, we discovered that the children's positions had changed. So we dispensed with the paper-and-pencil recording of children at play and decided that it had best be done with movie film. If counts were necessary to the research, they could be taken from selected frames via editor or projector stop action. Most significantly, we came to realize how kids play so spasmodically. Movement. Lots of movement. That is what Friedberg saw at his construction site, and that is what is apparent in any natural setting. Look at play in a school yard, for instance, or just in the street. It will remind you of swarming bees every time.

Linkage also attends to another readily observable phenomenon, that children are attracted to enclosed spaces. They are attracted to places unintended for their presence: they are at home in Christmas gift boxes, at the dump in derelict autos; in the park they play underneath pedestrian bridges, below arching shrub borders or beneath benches ostensibly reserved for adults. In a good linked system, the jogs, recesses, and varying platform levels which serve erratic pattern play coincidentally form encapsulated spaces for more ordered activity—they become a jail, house, boat, or whatever else whimsy suggests. Moreover, the enclosures serve passive pursuits, being securable territories for sand piling, socializing, or simply respite.

By all this you should not infer that I mean linkage to stand as the only strategy for breathing stimulus potential into a play environment. That conclusion would presuppose both a fictional and an insulting limitation to the creative mind. Observational evidence backed up by a credible theory does, however, suggest that it is one trustworthy way.

Theory the Arbiter

In the thinking about other creations, regard the role of theory in the comparisons made between linked and traditional playgrounds. The superiority ascribed to the former turned on the issue of complexity and the Ellis guidelines, which give complexity operational meaning. Application of those guidelines can determine the best of the traditional equipment assortment—swings, for instance. The guidelines can also be used to evaluate linked systems themselves. This means of evaluating is important to digest in light of some popular touting of linkage over the traditional because the former looks modern and the latter old-fashioned. Many modern-appearing complexes are actually very simple, for they have been produced with little understanding of what makes a linked system work.

45

3.12 Whether these look modern or old-fashioned, all score out on the simple side when addressed by the Ellis guidelines.

An understanding of theory can help one predict the play value of any play environment, whether its components be naturally present, custom-designed, or plucked from a manufacturer's catalogue. Playgrounds have been our example, but the basic premise extends to any project type. While we maintain our earlier stress that the absence of theory is no excuse for deferring action, latch on to one, nevertheless, if handy. It can serve well as a referee.

Eyeball Calisthenic 3

OBSERVE CHILDREN AT PLAY to imagine how behavioral investigations can inspire design patterns. Watch kids playing in undesigned settings as trash piles, backyards, in the woods, on the beach, etc. Describe recurring tendencies, and note the attributes of the physical items that seem involved in the execution of those behaviors.

PONDER: How might the play-supporting attributes of the undesigned settings be expressed in a designed environment? Imagine a variety of creations reflecting each attribute as well as any number of attribute combinations.

REPEAT the exercise in a designed playground, firsthand or with movies or videotape playbacks. Note the different ways each piece is used. Pay special attention to usage beyond that ordinarily expected, particularly attempts which are not quite fulfilled because of equipment limitations. Then imagine how the equipment might be modified to either increase ways of usage or enable completion of the unfulfilled behaviors.

ADAPT the exercise to the observation of other kinds of behaviors in both undesigned and designed settings.

4

Designers and Park Users: More Uneasiness

Over a decade ago, sociologist William Michelson wrote an article, "Many People Don't Want What Architects Want." The title may be overstated for effect, but the findings are unvarnished: people often gain significant satisfaction from physical environments which designers scorn, and large numbers are dissatisfied with settings that typically garner design awards. Before turning to behavioral theories relevant to human interaction with physical places, let's first explore some theories on the behaviors of designers themselves.

Deciding What Is Good

While this book would have you work with facility users when developing planning criteria, that approach is resisted by many designers. The resulting flap is reminiscent of age-old debates in other professions on how one goes about determining "what is good." For example, moral philosophers have struggled with the question for centruies, locking themselves into two basic schools. There are "subjectivists" who look solely within themselves to

4.1 Designers make decisions impacting users.

discern right from wrong, some even offering that a simple "I do or do not like it" is enough to justify an action. Facing off against them are "objectivists" who search for sources outside the self to sanction actions, sources independent of human determination like a god or "natural law." The most doctrinaire contend that there are externally derived laws which not only they, but all people, must follow.

Many designers are cut from similar cloth. There are "elitists" who seem to have taken the oath of Ayn Rand's Howard Roark. In *The Fountainhead* he ranted: "*I* am the architect. *I* know what is to come by the principle on which it is built. We are approaching a world in which *I* cannot permit myself to live. Now you know why *I* designed Cortlandt." (Not being exactly your cheery morning-type person, lo if he hadn't also dynamited the bloody thing.) "*I* gave it to you. *I* destroyed it. *I* agreed to design Cortlandt for the purpose of seeing it erected as *I* designed it and for no other reason. That was the price *I* set for my work. *I* was not paid." The italics are mine. They show ten—count 'em—ten *I's* in this brief passage alone.

Like the moral subjectivist, the design elitist elects himself the exclusive source for decision making. No issue is beyond reach, least of all behavioral matters. Listen to the response of a well-known designer of glass-box houses to reports of psychological problems associated with living in glass-walled apartments: "The notion that too much light is bad for people is utter nonsense." (Why?) "The natural way of man is to go toward light." (How do you come by this declaration?) "*I've* never pulled a drape in my life."

Similar to the moral objectivist is a species of designer we might call the "ego cipher" who relies upon external sources to the extent of forfeiting any role for himself in influencing what is good—especially for others. One variety is so mesmerized by the poetic lilt of elitist proclamations that he becomes a lobotomized mimic and therefore, ironically, turns into a elitist himself. He may, however, remain a purified strain by bogging down each job with an inextinguishable quest for facts and figures. Finally forced to make a decision, he will offer as justification only that "the data made me do it." Finally, there is the romantic type who is so consumed by a visceral glow of bygone days when everyone was forced to be his own artisan to survive that he will lobby the public to design and build its own works without stopping to wonder if the public has the time or even the desire to do so.

The Reality Factor Revisited. Let's look further at some classic debates among moral philosophers, not to argue moral philosophy, but to expose parallel thought patterns among designers. The analogy is quite apt. Moralists are concerned with how

4.2 Users have varying priorities in mind.

people ought to act. In the sense of our submission that plans are predictions about how people will use a place, so are designers.

Some moralists have offered that the prepotent force behind an action is the pursuit of happiness. Ergo, behaviors are "good" in proportion to the degree to which they promote happiness and "bad" as they tend to contribute to the reverse. So far, so good. Now comes the trap question that opponents always ask: does not the promotion of happiness push for mere animal-like gratifications? This question is answered by the certain comment: human beings have faculties more elevated than animal appetites and, once made conscious of those higher faculties, will not regard as happiness anything which does not include their gratification. That generates the retort: are not some pleasures more desirable than others, and, if so, who is to place relative value upon them? That "triggers the grabber," as the stand-up comics say: of the two pleasures, if there be one to which almost all who have experienced both pleasures give a decided preference, that is the most desirable pleasure. It is the "greater happiness." Why? *The studious appraiser—the expert or professional, if you will—says so.*

It is one thing to postulate how people ought to act, quite another to gain their acceptance. For without acceptance on the part of the subjects touched by the claim, it will not be put into service. If that be the case, the postulation can be said to be ineffective. Calling himself an "empiricist," philosopher John Dewey saddled the greater-happiness notion with that fate. The notion just doesn't prove out in the real world. People do not routinely place blind trust in the judgments of experts. Dewey concludes that the greater-happiness philosophers have speculated so removed from understanding human drives that the outcome was inherently forecasted. Stated another way, they intellectualized in a void and superimposed goals upon a set of needs which the goals did not fit.

Dewey submits his devastating perception that moral guidelines found acceptable to the people over the course of history have always had a content near enough to reality to be no more than a consecration of some already accepted measure. Accordingly, he asks moralists to supply their thinking with a sense of issues which are presently significant to the people. Appending his historical note, he commands philosophers to weigh the consequences of what the people seek. Hence, Dewey is not simply imploring a ritualistic validation of the findings; he is after a substantive regard for the present significance. No more—but no less. Thereby, a moralist's work may stand a fighting chance of becoming effective.

Not unlike the greater-happiness philosophers, designers who consider themselves acquainted with the full range of

THOUGHT PROCESS ALTERNATIVES

A. In-House "Club" Version

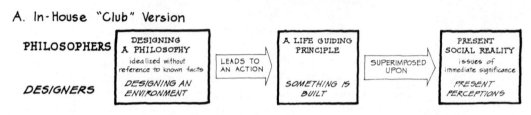

B. Internally Processing External Matter

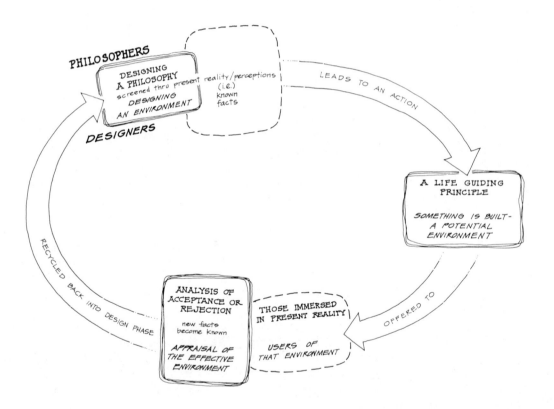

satisfactions gather in clubs to ascribe superiorities to environments. Much akin to the philosophers, they often end up modeling environments within the confines of self-perceptions. While the results may please their creators, cherished aspects often become ignored or abused by the laity. Although the temptation may have entered many minds, I am unaware of anyone who has actually reacted in a Roarkian manner and blown something up. More typically, when a designer is offended by signals of public dissatisfaction with a work, he will fault the user for insufficient application of intellect.

The gap between designers and users is further explained by the former's inattention to the statement of sociologist Herbert Gans:

> . . . a man-made artifact is [only] a *potential* environment and the perception of that man-made artifact in the culture is the *effective* environment. The effective environment may thus be defined as that version of the potential environment that is manifestly or latently adopted by its users. In one way, I am only restating the truism that an objective environment must be perceived subjectively before it affects behavior.

With only a bit of literary license, Fig. 4.3 transposes both Gans's and Dewey's thoughts into a graphic model that shows them to be quite alike. As a source for determining what is good, Gans and Dewey point to the perceptions of the subjects affected by the professional's work. Otherwise, moralists risk passing down only what moralists desire, and designers risk carving out environments containing merely what designers want.

Misdirected Paternalism

The trick for designers is to strike a middle ground between elitism and ego cipher. This necessitates a procession beyond self into the minds of others and then a return to an internal processing of those insights into responsive forms and arrangements, to the high level that a professional's training and experience permits. With that, it would be unfair to leave the impression that all environmental designers are either totally preoccupied with building monuments to themselves or seeking to hide from commitment. Indeed, the vast majority do strive to operate with user gain in mind, yet still too often in an unsuspecting fashion. As the car-washing example demonstrated, the subjects of many benevolences have not reacted in the grateful manner the designer had imagined.

Examples of good intentions gone awry are legion. In a San Francisco housing project, for instance, pains were taken to juxtapose a community center on the edge of the project which would be equally convenient to the project's tenants and the people from the neighborhood at large. It was expected that all would interact and a sense of community evolve. Additionally, to foster the making of friendships within the complex, the designer organized benches, shade trees, and other amenities at

THE SAN FRANCISCO
HOUSING PROJECT

• PEOPLE LOCATION

4.4 Contrary to the designer's expectations, these users chose to confine their friendship making to those sharing the inner courts.

a walk intersection in the center of the site. Both expectations were ignored. The tenants wanted no alliance with the neighborhood, which they perceived as so disreputable that they opted to mail in their monthly checks rather than to amble over to the rental office that the designer had planted in the community center. They also had no inclination to share intimacies with fellow tenants on an overall complex scale, preferring instead to develop friendships at the level of each apartment court.

The saving factor was that, despite the designer's misdirected attempts, the users were able to manage some satisfactions through the exercise of choice. Sometimes, though, attempts to solve one problem create other difficulties that are not so easy for users to work out on their own. Consider the discomforts brought upon the old cane-pole fishermen who were invited to the contemplation of ornamental plant material inserted by a designer to upgrade a sad-looking creek. The stuff soon grew so thick and thorny as to close off access to the stream and denied the elderly fishermen their habit of squatting near the water. The designer thought the trade off was in their favor, especially because he had provided benches in a more pleasant place. His was not an altogether unfounded surmise because the creek was polluted beyond the point of hospitality to your ordinary fish. The prospect of a catch, however, was an irrelevant point for the men; pretension was the key. As long as the old men maintained a constructive air about their presence, the police saw fit to leave them alone. But if they hunkered around benches in the middle of the place, harassment was going to be their lot, and no amount of scenic enrichment could provide compensation, however much it was meant as a move on their behalf.

Most disconcerting are design benevolences which have increased the aggravations which they were meant to settle down. This situation was the upshot with many vest-pocket parks started in the 1960's and early 1970's as resources for raising community pride in low-income neighborhoods and, among the residents, individual self-esteem. The goals and the vehicle chosen for attack were meritorious: rubble-strewn lots that were to be transformed into recreation spaces. The failings were less a matter of securing title (for philanthropists were often discovered who would lease the land for a token dollar or would donate holdings outright) than of tactics employed once the sites were in hand.

First, it was imagined that the world ran like a Pepsi commercial, in which pride flows automatically when people get together, hootenanny-style, to build a park. Neighborhoods, therefore, were hustled for voluntary labor. In many cases, few volunteers turned out, and these, hardly ever on a sustaining basis. Some also took to wondering why they were being called

4.5   There was a fragile détente between the old men and the cops as long as the former pretended to fish.

to build their parks while middle-class neighborhoods were having their recreation areas developed with city funds. Somebody eventually got the idea of paying unemployed residents for construction work. The wages offered, however, were so far below scales associated with similar work in town as to be embarrassing, and the lack of future to these jobs was equally hard to relish. Embarrassment turned to insult when residents were asked to maintain the places. The request was received as another menial assignment, reaffirming residents' perceptions of themselves as being eternally exploited and underemployed.

Commitments and enthusiasms turned out similarly marginal among many sponsors, especially when they were college students and professors whose involvements terminated with the academic term. Developments were abandoned in varying stages of completion, sites left to the mercy of weeds and otherwise worse-looking than in their earlier, "unimproved" state. Compounding the difficulties of turning out a labor force and seeing jobs through to completion were power struggles inadvertently brought about by the fact that most of the sponsors were middle class, Anglo, and white whereas the populations that they were trying to fire up were mostly poor, non-Anglo, and/or black. Unaccustomed to the politics of the street, many sponsors failed to secure the backing of community leaders. Their aggressive tendencies were thus taken as a threat to the positions that the leaders had carefully nurtured for themselves. Sometimes the whole project deteriorated into an exercise in choosing up sides.

What helped least of all was the hauling in of cast-off construction materials. Ecologically preoccupied at the time, the middle-class sponsors perceived splintery telephone poles, shopworn railroad ties, warped cable spools, chipped concrete culverts, and threadbare auto tires as exemplars of recycling. The poor saw the stuff literally to be junk, just another example of the dregs they felt accustomed to receiving from the city barrel.

In *Play and Interplay*, Paul Friedberg reacts to the early vest-pocket park movement with some thoughts on the underlying reasons for the rejections by the communities to be "enriched." In a deteriorating community, he says, "pride cannot be built with secondhand materials." If anything, a community with low morale "needs a facility that is better than elsewhere, unique, a place of distinction." He proceeds to offer an alternative, to use vest-pocket parks as a vehicle for helping low-income populations gain employable skills. For although doing your bit for ecology or linking arms with your neighbors may brighten some spirits, what erodes pride in poverty-stricken neighborhoods is low self-esteem stemming from poverty itself. To champion solutions which do not portend a way out of the poverty trap is to present a questionably effective opportunity for enhancing esteem.

4.6 The vest-pocket park movement often demonstrated that "free service is worth every penny."

55

Demythicizing Design Toward a
More Perfect Union

The shakers involved in the vest-pocket park movement deserve our gratitude even though many of their efforts went down the drain. Their pioneering attempts produced a legacy of lessons which designers have since consulted on their way to greater successes with similar work. Past design experiences are also laden with lessons that designers continue to ignore. There lingers, for instance, a persistent belief that upgrading the physical environment will unilaterally alleviate a host of humankind's ills—from crime and vandalism to peptic ulcers. This belief can be seen as an outflow from a designer's education. He spends so much time thinking in physical terms that if he sees a ticky-tacky subdivision as visually dull, he is prone to conclude that life in that environment must be equally deadening. To complete the equation, he goes on to imagine that if he were only to brighten up that setting, the people within would take to sparkling as well. I call this the "bollard delusion," after the row upon row of those concrete posts which serve no particular purpose, yet turn up in just about every neighborhood rehabilitation plan. As brought to you by the same friendly folks who postured that the conversion of downtown roadways into spiffy malls would suddenly increase sales, the formal term is *physical (or architectural) determinism*.

You can't blame designers for hoping. After all, physical enriching is what they do. Yet physical determinism remains empirically unsupported. On the contrary, using such quality-of-life yardsticks as crime rates and health levels, sociologist Michelson and planner Perin, among many others, have shown that where transformations from squalor to fine housing and open space have transpired, pathology may not only hold its own but occasionally increase in incidence.

Part of the declaration of an unbroken line between the kind of life one leads and one's physical surroundings is the claim that behaviors will be ordered about by the material setting. Although we have exposed that as a fallacious generalization by our car-washing example and the San Francisco housing case, many designers still cling to this myth. In so doing, they contribute yet another increment to the gap which exists between themselves and the public. Like the chap who named the icy expanse Greenland, they go about attributing more to their work than will probably result.

This is not to deny a role for physical surroundings in life-quality prescriptions nor to suggest that they have no effect upon human behavior. The question is with the notion of exclusivity, the idea that the physical environment is *the* regulating force. Taking a note from Dewey, it behooves us to examine what is known about human drives for a more realistic position. From that we may be better able to perform a service, diminish the gap between designers and users, advance the rate of predictive success, provide good design, be effective. They are all submitted as interchangeable terms. Take your pick.

Eyeball Calisthenic 4

OBSERVE PARTICULAR BEHAVIORS IN SPECIFIC SETTINGS to learn why people select or reject places for the performance of certain acts. As with the case of the campus "free speech area" described on p. 11, compare settings which have been designed to serve an activity, yet remain ignored, with places where that behavior regularly occurs.

PONDER: What attributes are missing in the ignored settings that routinely show up in the well-used places? How do those attributes support the behaviors observed?

5 | Behavioral Theories Impacting Design Routine

Threaded throughout our examples in Chapter 4 have been designers' attempts to fulfill what are commonly referred to as "basic human needs": for the housing project residents, a "sense of community" and "social interaction"; for the cane-pole fishermen, the sensory uplift of "aesthetics"; and for the poor, an enhancement of "self-esteem." In each instance, the objectives went unfullfilled because the users behaved differently than the designers expected. Often, the failure to do so is rationalized by reference to the inherent inconsistencies of human nature. That excuse could very well be a cue that the designer held an insufficient understanding of basic human needs from the onset. The needs themselves may exercise pulls that can, indeed, bring some consistency to human behavior.

Behavioral Formation, Human Needs, and User Priorities

Starting from scratch with the question of what underlies the formation of behaviors, we naturally turn to the sciences. But,

SOURCES FOR DECISION MAKING

SOMETIMES POLES APART

	Within Self	Beyond Self
Moral Philosophers	SUBJECTIVISTS	OBJECTIVISTS
Environmental Designers	ELITISTS	EGO CIPHERS
Behavioral Scientists	NATURE	NURTURE

as Fig. 5.1 demonstrates, we find that behavioral scientists are not about to be outdone by designers and moral philosophers in contradicting themselves. One camp believes in "nature" as the source of behavior, reasoning that we are products of biological imprinting, our behaviors ordered by genetically derived instincts. Believing thusly, ethologists (specialists in the study of animal behavior for whom imprinting is unquestioned) would say that their findings are readily transferable to human beings. Therapists, meanwhile, would have us "cope" with personal disturbances because the sources are independent of human determination.

The other camp believes in "nurture," contesting that findings from the study of animal behavior cannot be carried over to human beings, for humans are born unencumbered by imprinting and become products of their experiences. Sociologists stress that behaviors crystallize as a result of cultural influences. Allied therapists would beseech us to "unlearn" our hang-ups, for while cultural sanctions are a mighty force behind patterns of conduct, our responses were all learned to begin with. Nurturists have also had their say about cloning, maintaining that it will be impossible to duplicate human beings, as some imagine. They argue that what may start out as genetic Xerox copies will eventually individualize due to nonreplicable influences of the cultural environment.

Once more, a middle route like that offered by psychologist Abraham Maslow is recommended. He assumes that you accept that humans are animals on the highest link of the evolutionary chain. Yet, while holding to the idea that all mammals have common needs (acceding somewhat to the followers of nature), Maslow distinguishes humans from lower animals (acknowledging something from the advocates of nurture) by their advanced learning capacities. Learning complicates the lives of higher species in that they become faced with additional demands and the entertainment of choice.

In *Motivation and Personality*, Maslow gives this explanation. A lower animal (say, the rat) has few motivations other than to secure physiological necessities like sustenance, sex, body comfort, etc. As one goes up the animal scale (from rats to, say, monkeys and finally to humans), further needs emerge. Maslow classifies these postphysiological (or psychological) needs as (1) Safety-Security (stability, protection, freedom from fear, etc.), (2) Belongingness and Love (affection, striving to seek a place for group and family, need to identify with some external idea, etc.), (3) Esteem (a firmly based evaluation of oneself, respect and recognition of others, confidence in the face of the world). He terms all of these "deficiency motivations," but a final "growth" category, called (4) Self-actualizing (living up to one's potential), is sought not to fill a void, but for its inherent value.

Design Utility Problems of Basic Human Need Lists. One way in which designers have attempted to make human need theory operational in design is to brainstorm how satisfactions corresponding to each need category might be brought about by specific environmental amenities (look in the back of Perin's *With Man in Mind*, for example). While this would seem a commendable acknowledgment of the existence of basic human needs, there is the question about what need list to use. Maslow's is not the only one on the market. Note the inventory in Fig. 5.2 and the immediately apparent difference among them in size. Playwright-turned-behavioral-scholar Robert Ardrey claims that basic needs add up to three; Maslow says four (or five if you count the physiological); Alexander Leighton, calling his "essential striving sentiments" (which Perin uses), offers nine; Harvard psychologist Henry Murray refers us to thirteen; Peggy Peterson of Berkeley comes away with the grand prize for her list of twenty-five. Compounding the problem for the quick-study artist is comprehending what many of the items mean. From Murray's list, try "succorance," for instance. Indeed, it would appear that many of the items on the longer lists are not major entries at all, but subcategories of larger issues, as if one could expand or compress the whole like an accordion, depending

BASIC HUMAN NEEDS
according to :

Robert Ardrey	Abraham Maslow	Alexander Leighton *(Essential Striving Sentiments)*	Henry Murray	Peggy Peterson
SECURITY	SELF-ACTUALIZING	SEXUAL SATISFACTION	DEPENDENCE	HARMAVOIDANCE
	ESTEEM	EXPRESSION OF HOSTILITY	DEFERENCE	SEX
	LOVE and BELONGING	EXPRESSION OF LOVE	DOMINANCE	AFFILIATION
STIMULATION	SAFETY-SECURITY	SECURING OF LOVE	EXHIBITION	NURTURANCE
	PHYSIOLOGICAL NEEDS	EXPRESSION OF SPONTANEITY	HARMAVOIDANCE	SUCCORANCE
		SECURING OF RECOGNITION	INFAVOIDANCE	SECURITY
IDENTITY		ORIENTATION IN TERMS OF ONE'S PLACE...	NURTURANCE	ORDER
		SECURING & MAINTAINING OF MEMBERSHIP...	ORDER	FRAME OF ORIENTATION
		SENSE OF BELONGING...	REJECTION	SOLITUDE (PRIVACY)
		PHYSICAL SECURITY	SENTIENCE	AUTONOMY
			SEX	IDENTITY
			SUCCORANCE	EXHIBITION
			UNDERSTANDING	DEFENDENCE
				ACHIEVEMENT
				PRESTIGE
				AGGRESSION
				REJECTION
				DEFERENCE
				ABASEMENT
				PLAY
				VARIETY
				UNDERSTANDING
				MEANINGFULNESS
				SELF ACTUALIZATION
				AESTHETIC

upon how much precision is wanted. Moreoever, the lengthy lists are sure to evoke chicken-or-egg arguments about whether "exhibitionism," for instance, is a need or a means for fulfilling something else.

But let's say you overcome these quandaries. The problem then faced is to isolate what the physical environment can substantially touch. That may be done in a heady manner, as with our association of stimulation and play. Or it may simply involve common sense, as would be the case with the safety-security needs. The procedure is also to rule out items least likely to be satisfied through design. Thereby, we can avoid trying to relate applications where most would find them hard to believe they exist. Consider, for instance, the designer who was aroused by the prospect of enhancing sexual satisfactions and insisted that special sensory treatments be given to doorways, for he fancied that they symbolized entry into the womb.

Further yet, a detailed level of selection is necessary to determine which of the design-relevant needs are actually present among the people to be served. Such a step is required by the fact that people pursue the fulfillment of basic needs with varying degrees of intensity. Indeed, the primary users of a particular place may not have some of the needs in mind at all.

This phenomenon is attributed by Maslow to the fact that drives to fulfill needs trend steadily away from "hungers" to "appetites" as species move up the animal scale. Since appetites are less coercive than hungers, they are vulnerable to a selective process. Thus, although there may be a universal list of needs for humans, in practice certain needs dominate one individual while others dominate someone else. Needless to say, the process is largely outside of an environmental designer's control. Much of it is due to something within the individual, which Maslow ascribes to the relative influence of the needs themselves. Note in Fig. 5.2 how he offers his need list in hierarchical fashion (with the implication that other lists ought to be sorted out in like manner). The physiological appear as a subset, followed by others up a ladder according to their potency. Maslow describes them as acting upon people along the following lines: the needs lower on the diagram exert stronger pulls than those higher up, which is especially demonstrable when a number of needs are frustrated. The physiological needs are strongest of all. If they are substantially unfulfilled, they block out recognition of all other needs. If, say, a person has been continually defeated in securing sustenance, the drive to gratify that need will dominate his every action to the extent that, using Maslow's words, "no other interest exists except food and it can truly be said that this man lives by bread alone." Securing food even affects his view of the future. Utopia is imagined simply as a place where there is plenty of food. As for freedom, community spirit and

other qualities by which some poets have been known to characterize Utopia, they will not strike a receptive chord. Indeed,
for the person hung up on a lower rung of the Maslow ladder,
higher needs are not perceived to exist.

But when there comes the time that a hunger-driven person's belly becomes filled with some regularity, the next set of
needs pops into view. Safety-security quests take over. When
they are reasonably satisfied, the need to belong and be loved
rises up, and the person's habits and perceptions go into action
as love-making tools. Everything looks less important than being
loved, even physiological and safety-security needs. Since these
lower needs have achieved a relatively stable state, they become
underestimated, and temporary deprivations are tolerated.
Hence lower-need satisfactions may be traded off for gains
associated with the higher quest. Upon experiencing a significant measure of love fulfillment, the esteem needs are released
into play. And only after they have been tended to consequentially may self-actualizing begin to take hold.

A field version of brainstorming on the relationship of the
physical environment to basic need satisfactions is found in
landscape architect David Myhrum's thesis, *The Street as a Human
Resource in the Urban Lower-Class Environment*. With a need list as a
focusing device (he uses Ardrey's Big Three), Myhrum searches
for observable behaviors which allegedly reflect the pursuit of
each item of Ardrey's inventory and subsequently suggests how
to accommodate those behaviors in design. While the list may
suffice as a means for ordering thoughts, the process fails if
you must actually believe that what you observed is an expression of fulfillment in the need category in which it is placed. It is
simply impossible to determine what needs are being fulfilled
without having conducted an intensive and highly personal
analysis of the person involved.

Even card-carrying behavioral scientists are wary of attempting such correlations in light of the well-developed notions
that behavioral formation is a multideterminant process and that
basic human need pursuit is only one explanation underlying
recurring behaviors. Maslow himself would include as determinants not only the person's character (need) structure, but also
cultural influences and factors stemming from an immediate
condition. Moreover, the determinants are all so interwoven that
it is extraordinarily difficult to tie a behavior cleanly to one (such
as need structure alone), much less to any facet (as a particular
need). For instance, in Chapter 6, we will examine Edward Hall's
idea that people space themselves apart at regular intervals
when conducting certain kinds of transactions. Upon observing
such behavior, we cannot offhand determine if it is a manifestation of the love or safety-security need. In some degree, it could
be both. Or, as they say on the multiple-choice exams, it might

be none of the above, for it could just as well be a response learned from the subjects' culture or, simpler yet, a reflect reaction triggered by one person sidling up to another. Such behavior could also involve some combination of factors from the major categories, as in the instance of behaviors resulting from the pursuit of a basic need but in a manner fostered by acculturation.

A Questionable Run with Specifics, Yet Useful Generalizations. The foregoing has been to show why I think it futile for designers to bog themselves down in search of precise ties between behaviors and basic need fulfillments. The general lessons associated with human need theory are very rewarding, however, for they directly impact design routine. The concession that behavioral formation is a multideterminant process, for instance, should do away with the belief in single explanations as physical determinism. But the most telling revelation is that people rank order needs and not atypically in a hierarchy so unshakable that a designer stands little chance of causing the order of needs to be rearranged.

Going back for a moment to basic need inventories for purposes of demonstration, consider the matter of aesthetics. This need appears on many lists. Most designers place environmental beauty in the highest reaches of need gratification. Some apparently dedicate their careers to its provision. As one giant in the field proclaims: "My purpose is to extend the values art can offer into all crevices of human existence." Yet, when you get down to cases, you should not expect that aesthetics will be similarly valued by others whose moves toward aesthetic fulfillment thwart the fulfillment of deeper needs. You should not be surprised to discover that residents of high-crime areas will trade away the "mysteries of shadowy spaces" for a clear view or that children will make a fragile design "unbeautiful" in their quest for stimulation or that car washers will sacrifice visual tidiness for the chance to be seen or that cane-pole fishermen will pale at the prospect of harassment despite the new handsomeness of their fishing area.

5.3 People may have different perceptions of the same object: a horticultural wonder or a hiding place for muggers?

The point is not to rule out aesthetic gratification as a basic need, much less to go back on my previous statements on beauty as a requisite quality of good design. The argument is against refusing to meet the user on his own terms, against the lack of *parallel attention* to the user's more highly rated and more immediately significant goals. A residential area can be made beautiful without surveillance being obstructed. Stimulating play structures can be visually appealing or clumsy-looking. A handsome car-washing corral can either be hidden or well within view of others, and, for sure, there are many ways to beautify a creek. With simultaneous attention to other needs, it may be said that "a designer can have his artifact and eat it too."

If such cherished aspects as aesthetics are not valued highly by users in specific instances, lay off the insufficient application of intellect routine and the usual clubhouse declarations that follow to "educate" the public to "appreciate" what is being done on its behalf. Where an elevation of sights is imagined to be in order, harken back to the Maslow postulation that it is need gratification on one level that releases a being for the pursuit of gratifications on another, the lower needs taking precedence when a number are frustrated. Better the efforts be put to fulfilling the "lower" needs, for it could cause the "higher" ones to pop more quickly into view.

Be Situation-Specific. If he is unattuned to users' priorities, a designer chances delivering his all to a nonvisible need and, more critically, leaving significant needs unmet. There have been occasions when the results of his inattention have been tragic. The classic case on record is a huge St. Louis housing project, notorious because it had to be leveled a decade after its erection: people refused ouright to live there. Contributing to the debacle was the design stroke that led to the installation of elevator entries on alternate floors. Those who lived on the nonentry floors had to move through two hallways and an intervening stairwell to get to their units. Since this routing would increase the chances of meeting neighbors, once again it seemed that social interaction and the building of community togetherness would be served. The greater need, however, was for security. Gangs of toughs found it more convenient to turf off hallways in the high-rise structures than in the outside spaces many floors below. However, interact with the residents they did, shaking them down, mugging them, and catching them in crossfires as the residents ran the gauntlets to their doors.

To localize the thinking about hierarchies to specific populations (for inevitably, they are what a designer must deal with), many analysts have shifted from speaking about all-encompassing basic human needs to the simpler, *user needs*. That shift also lessens the tedious and often impossible demand on designers to classify behaviors. They can record users' preferences on their merits and in whatever terms seem appropriate. The shift in vocabulary notwithstanding, the essential lesson of basic need theory remains operational for outlining the designer's task: try to satisfy everything on the users' list, and if that proves impossible, pay the most generous attention to the items users rank at the top.

Presently, it is safest to investigate user needs case by case, for the few generalizations available are mostly of an unsophisticated sort. One must also remain wary of exceptions to any common rule. From some studies which have attempted to generalize rankings, however, interesting comparisons have come to light which not only reinforce the theme of perpetual clash between designers and users, but also show that different user groups can be far apart. Planner Clare Cooper, for instance, has gathered enough data to assure us that "noninstitutionality" ranks near the top among user needs with the poor who reside in public housing. Change the population group to the middle class, and sociologist Suzanne Keller indicates that "spaciousness" is more highly regarded in residential environs. For neighborhood park development, landscape architect Randy Hester reports that design professionals tend to emphasize the importance of activity settings whereas nondesigners are more concerned about the kinds of people who use the place. Further breaking down the categories of park users, Hester found that the elderly have a major concern for safety but that middle-class college students, more interested in communing with nature, placed safety way down on their list.

One person's means for fulfilling a priority need may also be found to be quite different from another's. Take status seeking, for example. To one individual, as we have demonstrated, it may be satisfied through the conspicuous ownership of an automobile. But to another it may be satisfied through a display of attire, to a third through the maintenance of a leadership role (say, a role in the forefront of the ecological movement which might lead one to impose recycled materials on playgrounds for disenfranchised neighborhoods), or to a fourth, more simply yet, through acquisition of membership in just the right club. Indeed, status may even be assured by owning a goat. That is precisely what one designer discovered to be at the heart of users' dissatisfactions with the multistory residential units he had created to replace a Caribbean shantytown. The goat was a symbol of societal stature. Although the new dwellings were decidedly more sanitary than the earlier shacks, that fact could not compensate for the residents' inability to tether a beast outside of their door, in the corridor of a third-floor flat.

5.4 Means for fulfilling the same need may differ among people: expressing status, for instance.

5.5 Professional acculturation: Designers are inclined to emphasize differences in visual detailing when individualizing places.

The Effects of a Designer's Acculturation

The idea that individuals rank their needs and accustom themselves to specific means of fulfillment extends to designers. Of course. Designers are humans too. Therefore, when designers question tendencies to rate activity settings over the kinds of people who use a place or look lightly upon displaying a car, much less a goat, they would do well to consider how many of the priorities which they assign to their works are objectively derived. Conceivably, the designer's priorities may reflect the designer's need structure and the culture in which he received his learning, and they may, therefore, turn out to be unwelcome interventions in the lifestyle of others with another acculturated point of view.

Such subjective interventions can have professional or personal roots. An example of the former is found in one of Cooper's public housing cases. The case starts off admirably with the designer's receptivity to noninstitutionality as a leading criterion. Economics mandated row housing, so the designer proceeded to individualize each unit by following the custom of his discipline in varying colors, stoop designs, roof overhangs, and railing configurations. The residents were not impressed. How outrageous! What eventually brought solace to many were a design addendum that gave each a fenced-off space at the rear of the unit and a management policy that allowed residents to use and adorn the space as they saw fit—not visual detailing, but the proprietary use of space did the trick.

A personal bias intervention is the nub of our ubiquitous car-washing case. The designer grew up in suburbia; there the house rather than the car is the presiding status symbol, and the front yards serve mainly as manicured settings for framing the dwellings. Suburban neighborhood activity is predominantly selective—barbecues and the like by invitation only—and it all takes place in backyards. Result: his design for the inner-city residents became a big "put-on." Recall Fig. 2.4, and compare it to Fig. 5.6 nearby. Note how the designer applied aspects of a design solution which nicely supported his manner of living to a dissimilar style of life.

THE SUBURBAN STREETSCAPE

• *PEOPLE LOCATION*

5.6 Personal acculturation: Those who grow up in suburban settings may be accustomed to socializing at the rear of their dwellings, not in the front.

Neighborhood Parks. In his papers on recreational trends at the neighborhood level, Seymour Gold frequently cites planning at odds with consumer lifestyles as one reason why many developed sites lie vacant much of the time. The problem may reside in producers' personal attachments to the neighborhood-park concept itself. The standard by which most planners operate tells us that a 15-to-20-acre site serves local recreation needs—one neighborhood, one park, in the fashion of a Supreme Court ruling. The opposite idea is several, smaller parcels—the vest-pocket parks. One faction of the producers resists the latter with the claim that maintenance costs increase. Be that as it may (and it may well be), those taken by Gold's citation might question why funds are put to maintaining places that are rarely used, why good is thrown after bad. Some producers also claim that vest-pocket parks cause a spreading out of noise and nuisance, and that may be true as well. Yet, one person's noise and nuisance may be another's liveliness and delight—which returns us to the issue of disparate perceptions.

To centralize facilities or distribute them across the neighborhood map is the question. Hypothetically for the moment, if we sift that through a user perspective, neither the traditional standard nor the vest-pocket idea comes out right or wrong—except as one is chosen independent of the leisure patterns of the service population. Perhaps what we need is a new planning concept, one that bases the decision to centralize or scatter upon a reading of what those leisure patterns happen to be. It is primarily a consideration for fresh developments and rehabilitation efforts where parcels of varying size exist. Although the matter may be moot in built-up areas where site selection is severely restricted, even there attention can be given to traditionally fallow spaces like cul-de-sac centers or the oversized reaches between sidewalk and curb. (See Pinfold's thesis for other possibilities as well as a systematic appraisal of selected leisure patterns.)

As for criteria to launch that concept, first some speculating, then an introduction to an actual case. The least-used parks of a centralized sort seem to be in places where a fear of harm from others on the street keeps people at home. That fear often makes parents keep preteens near the nest so that they don't come under the influence of negative role figures like dopers, gang leaders, or simply characters whose dress or conduct is too "exotic." A sprinkling of small places convenient to household windows might just be the ticket, especially where private backyards are scant and streetside traffic is part of the neighborhood social fabric.

Understanding children's leisure patterns could also influence the decision about what kind of park best suits their needs. It has been noted by many researchers as well as casual observers that much of children's play takes place in brief episodes—

5.7 A housing project with play spaces decentralized throughout the neighborhood.

between school and the evening meal, after supper for a few minutes before dark, etc.—in the nearest vacant lot, on a front stoop, sidewalk, or street, and less often in The Park a few blocks distant. No wonder. Kids aren't dumb. Time is precious. Why waste any in travel? Public housing studies like Cooper's have narrowed down the play area considered desirable by pointing out that tots always seem to play within a small radius of the most frequently used entrance to the home. This fact has led some adventuresome public-housing planners in St. Paul to spot clusters of playground apparatus along pedestrian ways associated with those entrances rather than to gather them all up in one corner of a 15-to-20-acre chunk somewhere down the street.

On the other hand, where fear of others is not notably present, or, indeed, where contact with "exotic characters" might be desired by parents for their youngsters as a lesson in life, and, of course, where the neighborhood manner relegates the streetscape to passive showcase status, one large centralized place may work out best. Some combination of plans may also be in order: if people play competitive team sports requiring a large field, designers can provide one in a central location as well as distribute small spaces for play near home or spontaneous play.

A blue-ribbon example of leisure lifestyle analysis as the foundation for park planning is provided by landscape architect Bill Taylor and researcher Susan Stone who drew up a recreation plan for a midwestern urban area that was programmed for renewal. As described in their report, *Inner City Turnaround*, and excerpted by Taylor in the September 1978 issue of *Landscape Architecture* magazine, their study is noteworthy if not inspirational for revealing lifestyle patterns with simple observational techniques.

Their curiosity piqued by the near-total absence of people in the existing neighborhood park, Taylor and Stone drove up and down the streets, recording on a map where the residents actually were during typical leisure hours. Yet the researchers grew jumpy at feeling they were constantly followed. As it turned out, their research ploy—cruising the neighborhood— was also the pervasive means of recreation in the place. All age groups were involved. On foot or by auto, knots of young adults traveled particular blocks "looking for the action," as one resident put it. Youngsters rode bikes, hot wheels, and trikes on sidewalks and minimally trafficked streets, and everyone stopped now and again to socialize. Meanwhile, oldsters took it all in from front porches erected as if they were bleachers for those interested in watching the events.

Successfully resisting their suburban, middle-class inclinations to stuff the major park, Taylor and Stone translated their insights into a plan which peppered not only play structures,

5.8 The Camping Exam: Which depicts the best camping environment?

but basketball courts, garden plots, and a whole range of recreational features throughout the neighborhood. These separate spots were linked up by having the most popular cruising sidewalks (not the back alleys) widened, and clusters of seats were added along the way. And, oh yes, as for car-washing corrals, they too were plotted into the plan—off the streets—but still within view of lots of people's natural congregating spots.

Camping. Although leisure pattern analyses are most readily applicable to neighborhood planning, they may be equally consequential far beyond the neighborhood scene. Take campgrounds, for instance. Let us begin with a test. (It's obviously a trap but humor the author and play along.) Refer to Fig. 5.8 and select from illustrations A, B, and C the one which, *in your estimation*, depicts the best camping environment.

While the computer is tabulating the results, let me submit that, like the thinking that produces only a single model for neighborhood parks, it is not uncommon for planners to believe that a camper is a camper is a camper and, therefore, one campground can be pretty much like the next. Once upon a time it might have been that campers were of like bent, in the sense that they were all attracted to the out-of-doors and wanted to meet the wilderness on its own terms and for what it inherently offered. Now, return to your choice. If you selected "A," I suspect you lean in that direction. Relative to the other choices, "A" appears to possess the greatest potential for satisfying that urge. Let's call you and others like you, present-day "Thoreauites." At the same time, if you are involved in planning or policy, I must also ask, do you strive to capture the "A" campground image in all of your works and are you totally repulsed by the conditions typified by illustration "B"? Furthermore, in reflecting upon the possible intrusion of acculturated bias, don't cast off alternative "C" as the joke it may seem to be. Over the years that I have been presenting these choices, "C" has received only one vote, but á telling one: from a building architect who grew up in New York City. Would you care to have him plan your campground fully loose on a déjà vu trip?

In contrast to the Thoreauite, another version of boondocks-goer has cropped up over the last couple of decades. This "Social Camper" brings his neighborhood lifestyle with him. Much of it comes in physical form: lawn chairs, motobike, radio, not to mention T.V. He also brings his activities: cracking the six pack, watching the ball game, throwing lawn darts, gabbing with neighbors, laying a steak on the hibachi, and if the kids get underfoot, shooing them off to the playground or store. It would seem that camping here means relaxing in accustomed ways without being pressured to mow the lawn or paint the house, pressures felt if the holiday is spent at home. As we have mentioned, camping may also be a status-gratifying operation that focuses on the style and complexity of the camping rig. Note now often the rig comes complete with sign announcing hometown and names of family members as handles for generating conversation and how, occasionally, Chinese lanterns get strung along awnings for attention-getting at night. As for the inherent offerings of nature, they serve simply as the backdrop against which it all gets played.

A third version of camper is the "In-Betweener," whose special dilemma is that he has traits of both the Thoreauite and the Social Camper, but is neither. The In-Betweener prefers not to abstain entirely from his urban-suburban routine, such as doing without a daiquiri before dinner, but is offended by forced confrontations with display and clatter. On the other hand, while he gravitates toward the natural experience, he does not have the resolve to go all the way.

5.9 Campers vary; so, too, should campgrounds.

The Thoreauite

The Social Camper

The In-Betweener

71

Campers come in at last these three versions. So, too should campgrounds, and they should not do so only in the sense of whole parks being put in the service of one or the other. Attention should be given to providing *a variety of arrangements for every overnight park.* A variety would seem especially appropriate near urban centers, where competition for satisfying settings is most severe. Each part of the arrangement should be distinguished by design characteristics and programs suited to the particular lifestyle for which it is intended. And to avoid perceptual conflicts, each part should be strictly segregated from the other.

As for the design characteristics of these parks, I can only speculate. The thumbnail sketches drawn in Fig. 5.9 are obviously superficial; in-depth studies with design-relevant conclusions have not yet been done. A couple of things seem quite clear, however. Plumbing (pit privies versus flush toilets), transportation mode (drive to versus walk in), and habitation type (tent versus recreation vehicle), which are traditional criteria for characterizing campgrounds, will not suffice. Habitation type is especially suspect as a camping lifestyle indicator, for observations indicate that people's penchant for socializing as opposed to experiencing nature privately are not commensurate with the kind of roofing people bring. One relevant factor is the degree of visual separateness sought by campers. Those who come to absorb nature may want to be strictly separated from their brethren in order that repeated contacts not detract from the private enjoyment of it all. To submit a Social Camper to the Walden-like "A" environment, however, may create equal frustration, for the Social Camper is fulfilled by the close and constant contacts which "B" affords. Here is yet another version of see-and-be-seen which, in decisions about site orientations and distancing, designers may materially affect. As for the poor In-Betweener, the designer can place him near enough to neighbors to assuage his urban-induced insecurities, yet by judicious screening with topography and plant massing isolate him enough to reduce contact demands. Control over the see-and-be-seen is left predominantly up to the In-Betweener.

Searching for the Interface Between Design and Behavior. This business about user needs, priorities, perceptions, and satisfactions is context material out of which we now rescue and pinpoint and term "behavior." Hereafter, we will also be focusing less upon what the state of the art does not allow us to understand than on what is known.

Behaviors are actions. They are the things which people do physically. Design is also physical by outcome, delivering forms that you can kick and that go bump in the night. Accordingly, design can either facilitate or hinder the execution of behaviors, and in the most literal sense. Friedberg's linked-up forms facilitated play in random patterns; the plant masses on the bank of the sad-looking creek hindered access to the water.

We have stressed that there are many forces which interact to shape behaviors. It is conceivable that all may not have equivalent clout. In particular cases, one force, while falling short of being an exclusive determiner, may evolve as the primary force, with the others contributing in tangential ways. That brings us to the question: what is the likelihood of that primary force being the physical place?

Some who would champion the primacy of design may point to correlations that have been drawn between aberrant behaviors and closed environments like underwater sea labs and space capsules. They might also cite the influence of physical surroundings on individuals in the form of phobias like acrophobia (which might be precipitated by one's finding oneself on a fiftieth-story balcony) or claustrophobia (induced by encapsulation in the elevator that got one to that balcony). But with respect to environmental design practice, it must be noted that the cited closed environments are controlled settings and uncharacteristic of public spaces, where the influencing variables are seldom so few in number. Phobias are too individualistic for wholesale consideration except as they apply in settings where afflictions are known to be common to the user group. In mental hopitals, for instance, paranoid patients, who are preoccupied with marking off personal boundaries, have been driven to the brink by round dining tables and have resorted to defiantly rearranging the table paraphernalia. Square tables, however, tend to be more placidly shared because their corners do much of the delineation automatically.

Although designers should not discount the contribution of physical arrangements and detailing in recognized therapeutic routines, in the more typical day-to-day circumstances which they face, designers are left with only the simplistic postulation that if they put down a walk and wall it on both sides, people will move exactly as the design dictates. See, the postulation goes, the physical facility was preeminent in ordering the behavior. Questions: Will that notion prove true where people are free to behave otherwise—as at the San Francisco housing project where the designer's attempt to order interaction was snubbed. Where the notion does "work," could other forces have created a desire which the wall-walk combination merely coincided with? And, most consequentially, where it works, in the sense of forcing actions against people's preferences, will the design be happily received or will it fuel aggravations like those reported by psychologist Robert Sommer in his examination of a California urban park?

Contending that this downtown site was not receiving what planners call its "highest and wisest use" because it was catering to the old men who frequented it, Sommer reported,

5.10 The pensioners desired to sit apart from the winos, but that was rendered impossible when all had to compete for the shady portions of stationary seats.

city officials determined to "open the park" for use by others. Their objective was to eliminate the "ominous crowd look" caused by the old-timers massing around clusters of moveable benches. In pristine testimony to physical determinism, their idea was to disperse the benches along walks at long intervals and to lock them in with concrete. See, spreading out the facilities will spread out the users as well. The upshot of the change actually was to intensify the crowd look. Whereas previously the benches could be scattered under shade trees, the same number of users now draped themselves over the few stationary benches that at any one time avoided the broiling summer sun. Moreover, Sommer discovered that the old men were of two sorts, pensioners and alcoholics, who were now led to compete for a diminished number of choice locations. That competition created an antagonizing mix, for the pensioners desired to keep the winos at an appropriate social distance.

Here, or in the more devastating St. Louis high-rise case, what is served by putting users through that kind of aggravation?

Actually, I find arguments over the primacy of physical design in shaping behaviors to be tiresome. Since enlightening data are skimpy to nonexistent, responses to questions like those I've posed usually wind up as circular debates or trigger so much defensive rhetoric as to blind people to a more immediately fruitful course. That course begins with an acknowledgment of what has come to be known around my shop as "Al's Heresy." Considering how often users act contrary to physical cues when they are able to exercise choice, I would submit that the physical environment is the least potent of the forces which may determine behavior. At the same time, however, it would not be inconsistent to say that physical environment may *encourage* a behavioral response not unlike the way in which the aesthetic qualities of a design have potential for generating a sensory response.

Undermining this analogy is another professional bias regarding aesthetics. When it comes to describing environments, design vocabulary is so riddled with life-state terms, like "gloomy," "peaceful," "exhilarated," "dulling," etc., that it makes places sound animate. Physical objects such as trees, pavement materials and water forms, which designers choose in the interest of providing a peaceful mood, become spoken of as themselves becalmed. The people on the scene are subject to the same fallacy.

A place has no life in and of itself. When a designer manipulates aesthetic qualities for the purpose of creating a mood, he merely offers a message which must be processed by a person (or as Gans has reminded us, "be perceived subjectively") in order for the mood to take hold. The possibility of success is enhanced if the subject is not so preoccupied as to ignore messages from the environment; it is decreased if his preoccupations are contrary to the atmosphere suggested by the place. I question, for instance, the probability of a "peaceful" setting automatically easing the jitters of some cheat who is deliberating the no-win case he must shortly present for audit by the I.R.S. But it would seem that the mood-message has the best chance of capturing an individual if his mind is in harmony with a setting's aesthetics. If our friend with the I.R.S. problem is actually seeking respite, odds are he'll find it in a place with peaceful qualities, very much as the designer intended.

The same things can be said of behaviors. Just as designers ought not to believe that everyone surrounded by an aesthetic web will yield to it, they should not believe that an action necessarily will be triggered by the presence of a physical work. Similarly, it follows that people behave as designs encourage when the designs lend support to a sought-after goal, or, further paraphrasing Dewey, when a design is a consecration of some already accepted measure.

For the designer as predictor, the assignment changes from one of trying to anticipate what a design will determine to trying to anticipate *what already has been determined before design gets underway.* We loosely term these predetermined tendencies "habits," and you need only consult your own mannerisms for examples which physical design can touch. Are you a front-door or a back-door person, for instance? My parents were intransigently back-door people, and for reasons deeper than mere convenience, for it was in their Eastern European tradition to route family traffic by way of the back door while reserving the

5.11 Who uses what door of your house, and why? Do you have other habits which your physical environment support?

streetside entry and adjoining front room for guests. Architect Christopher Alexander discovered a similar habit among Peruvians. In Peru it is not only traditional to entertain in the parlor, but it is considered respectful of those walking through the parlor to join the company. A second entrance well away from the parlor therefore became mandatory for family members to use routinely in order to avoid happening upon guests whom they'd rather avoid. A visitor must also be offered munchables and no excuse is acceptable. But the offering must be shorn of fuss. The out-of-sight entrance thus is doubly important. For if the guest should drop in when the cupboard is bare, someone in the household can secretly leave for the bakery and return without the visitor being aware.

Design as Servant. Herbert Gans prefers the word "predispositions" to "habits". Its use begs the issue of behavioral formation in avoiding allusions to human needs, cultural derivation, situational reactions or combinations thereof. That avoidance is also its strength for designers. Considering how often root causes remain obscure, for designers to think simply of predispositions is as pragmatic as moving from worrying about human to user needs.

Gans asks us to regard highly the satisfactions which accrue when the physical environment permits predisposed behaviors to be carried out. In fact, it is his considered opinion that people's greatest displeasure with the designed environment can be traced to its inadequate supporting of their established routines. In Levittown, New Jersey, for example, Gans discovered that the most highly satisfied residents had a predisposition toward privacy that was well served by the subdivision's low densities and homogeneous land use. Dissatisfied Levittowners, in contrast, were the more gregarious people who remained unfulfilled by such adaptive strategies as "koffee klatching" or modifying the physical environment. (Ever try rearranging a subdivision on your own?) Gans noted that residents of Boston's West End, in diametric contrast, were predisposed toward maintaining kinship associations, a predisposition nicely accommodated by the neighborhood's tightly intermingled patterns of streets, housing, and commercial facilities which kept everyone within hailing distance of each other. Then the West Enders were uprooted through urban renewal. Among those forced into the suburbs, where the land use constrained spontaneous mingling, nearly half suffered "fairly severe grief." After two years, over a quarter of the female population was still "depressed."

From this we may infer that the execution of predisposed behaviors is a kind of user need and that it can rank high on a user's priority list. We may also infer that design can act effectively as a *servant to predispositions*.

Activity Issues: Digging Below the Surface with Plaza Design.
Behavioral predispositions fall into two categories—people's overt activity preferences and a sociopsychological agenda. The *overt activity preferences* are familiar now to designers, and especially recreation planners, to whom it is second nature to survey people about the things they wish to do in parks. This category deserves attention here for the nuances that sometimes get overlooked. Survey results may repeat themselves so often that they become ritualized, and idiosyncratic exceptions ignored. Designers expect the elderly for instance, to strike a decided preference for shuffleboard and horseshoes. I know of one designer who decided to skip the activity assessment on a park meant to serve an elderly population because the findings developed by others were good enough for him. But the shuffleboard courts and horseshoe pits which he subsequently installed were never used. He later discovered from an elderly relative who happened to live nearby that most of the elderly users spent their winters in Florida and returned to the park in the summer seeking only some shaded spots, attractive surroundings, and comfortable seats to nestle in and swap stories. They had a running joke, both spoken and enacted, that having had their fill down south, they couldn't care less if they ever saw another shuffleboard court or lifted another horseshoe again.

In a survey taken among another group of elderly, in this case Italian men, bocci was preferred. Horseshoes was of only minor interest, and shuffleboard was nowhere on the chart. Soccer was also important to the elderly men. Although only younger males actually played soccer, the elders' conversations (at the barbershop) and their betting revealed the rabid competition among teams sponsored by local businessmen. Especially because teams represented different neighborhoods, the older men took extraordinary pride in games and attached great meaning to having, "by God," the best local facility in town.

Discerning people's idiosyncrasies also bears upon how designers provide "open space," which shows up on site as a vacant reach and in which they assume that "free play" or "spontaneous use" will take place. Although, by definition, spontaneity would seem to defy prediction, designers still ought to have a sense of options most likely to be taken by the user population (frisbee throwing, pick-up street hockey, *tai chi* exercising, penny pitching, and what you will). If not, they may leave users with an open space of a size, shape, and surface inadequate for the options chosen. There are certainly cases in which users are best served by a designer leaving a space alone. But whenever I see vacant areas on a plan labeled "free play" or some such, I often wonder if the designer has moved in the interest of flexibility or is simply covering up the absence of any idea whatsoever about the activities which might go on in that

5.12 Was "open space" labeled on the plan without forethought to how it might be used?

space. He may have crossed the line between serving a host of behaviors and serving none satisfactorily at all.

I have the same suspicion about the design of plazas and the large, undifferentiated spaces which most contain. Except for some sketchy references to walking through or sitting down, plaza development programs are notoriously short on overt activities. Most end up programmed to show off a sculptural artifact or become artifacts themselves, to be experienced in the same detached manner as paintings on a museum wall. That development is quite ironic in light of the significant activity considerations which paralleled the showcase dimension in historic examples after which many contemporary plazas are modeled. Venice's Plaza San Marco, for instance, is on everybody's all-star list of fine plazas. One reason for its excellence is the sensitive manner in which its bell tower is held in fragile equilibrium by the grand volume of space in which it stands. But we should also recognize how well that very same space was suited for the religious extravaganzas produced in their time as counterreformation ploys. St. Peter's Square is another vast space of such overwhelming scale as to strike awe if not utter humility in the breast of the beholder in symbolic testimony to the greater power present. Not coincidentally, it is also an accommodating expanse for mass papal audiences.

Many contemporary plazas are fashioned after Old World town squares or the Spanish missions, which brought the plaza concept to the American West. Originally, they too were designed as marshaling areas for religious ceremonies. They also served as places for farmers to display their goods, and the missions' ever present fountains were the sole sources of water. Arbitrary replications of their forms and details for contemporary circumstances, however, may produce socially irrelevant misfits not unlike the one produced by the chap who superimposed the suburban solution on the urban streetscape. Yet today it seems as if the Old World squares were franchised and that one has only to dial an 800-number to get one, too. Plazas that are carbon copies of Spanish missions routinely crop up, not just in historic districts, where they make sense, but in swinging-singles apartment complexes and sport, convention, and government centers. In some cases, there is reason to argue that the plaza provides visual continuity with the surroundings or ties to a cherished past. But how about use? Each of the examples cited would appear to have different activity prescriptions, none of which may have anything to do with the traditional mission plaza where the users hawked vegetables, filled water jugs, washed undies, and engaged in Catholic rituals.

On the other hand, I once came upon a mission courtyard remnant which fronted a modern church. Only a plaque bore witness to the former courtyard. Its original surface had been given up in redesign for criss-crossed walks and grassy fragments with a few flower patches thrown in. It was Palm Sunday. Mass was preceded by palm distribution, readings, hymns, and plenary blessings. Banner-laden and brass-band accompanied, the ceremonies culminated with traffic stopping as the multitude flowed across the street to the door of the church. Once more down the irony trail, all of this occurred in a place once set up precisely for such a purpose, but a place now neutered by design to serve no particular purpose at all.

It is not that historic treatments are maladapted to all contemporary doings. Plazas which one saw religious gatherings may handle many modern festivals, political rallies, and protest demonstrations well. Flea markets and handicraft peddling have fit easily into places once used for produce display. But a designer who is going to replicate an earlier style ought to be armed with some evidence that such events may indeed take place. Moreover, he should be prepared to modify that earlier style to accommodate needs that either never existed in bygone days or were less pervasive.

Consider how seldom designers specify a modern use for the town-square fountain despite the fact that, as if by decree, a fountain always turns up in plaza design. The fountain is spoken of solely as a visual piece. Often it is *the* central feature, ordering all other decisions about the work. Let's say, though, that a plaza in question is surrounded by high-rise office buildings whose populations are given to brown-bag lunching. If, as was the rule in pre-bologna-sandwich days, a giant space has been created within which the fountain is to be fully experienced, and screening material has been disdained for adulterating the simplicity of the void, chances are that the plaza will be a wind tunnel in the fall and a heat sump in the summer. It is also likely to lack scaled-down spaces for comfortable group conversations. Seating will probably be limited to linear slabs, which may be oriented well for glimpsing the water, yet, as we will develop in Chapter 6, poorly suited for accommodating the postures struck when friends converse.

All is not woe, though. An alternative has come among us. It is the "participatory" fountain which affords users the opportunity to wade at will. These fountains are ranging complexes

5.13 The utilitarian, mission-courtyard fountain (above) often shows up in contemporary courts as an arbitrary artifact (below).

79

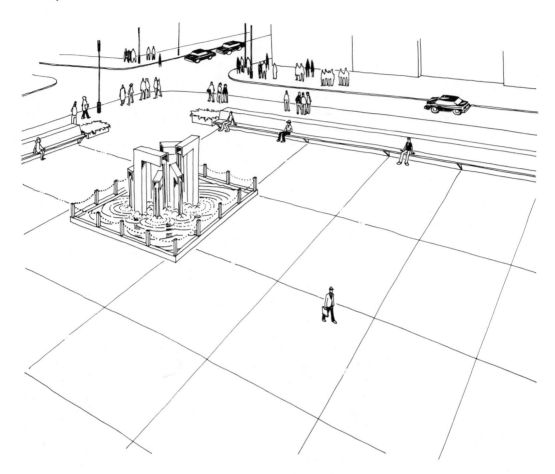

5.14 A question to be asked about a plaza designed to show off a fountain: Is it also a good place to eat lunch?

with access networks and sitting coves intermingled with water courses that rush, bubble, spurt, fall, pool, and anything else that traditional water features were ever called upon to do. As for places with historic ties, they pose no problem for the clever designer. I have seen them fit into central-city plazas in the Southwest without any debasing of their overall Old World flavor. Most notable, however, are the participatory waterworks found in several Portland, Oregon, plazas. Universally acclaimed as masterpieces of art, they are also great places to lunch.

Brown-bag lunching is just one use for the contemporary plaza. People watching and trysting must also be counted. Physical fitness activities may come to be another use. Such activities could lead to exercise courses smack in the heart of business and convention districts as more people turn from the three-martini lunch as a tension breaker to having a go at keeping in shape. Much more should be revealed via the continuing studies of people and plazas by that most resourceful of social analysts, William H. Whyte. Meanwhile, as is the case with parks in general, a lot remains to be discovered by watching how people use space.

5.15 The "participatory" waterworks: fountain design with contemporary use in mind.

Digging Further to Uncover Hidden Dimensions. The second form of behavioral predisposition comprises a *sociopsychological agenda* that may underlie overt activities. Variously ascribed to need gratification or social customs, sociopsychological needs are often tucked away in people's subconscious minds. Even if they are consciously apparent to the user, he may find them awkward to admit. Therefore they seldom show up in typical recreation preference surveys. We will specify how to discern both the presence and nature of the sociopsychological agenda in Chapter 7. Our purpose here will be simply to establish how pivotal its treatment may be in bringing about user satisfactions. The stage has already been set by our discussion of the see-and-be-seen phenomenon. In this chapter we noted it at work in the case of the Peruvian host-guest ritual where more was required in the house design than the provision of square footage to entertain.

Regard how consideration of this sociopsychological dimension can make a designer generate a plan significantly different from one which considers only activity preferences. Imagine, for instance, a program for a neighborhood park which we'll simplify for demonstration purposes into a playground, basketball court, and bocci green (see Fig. 5.16A). From an overt activity standpoint, the scheme seems reasonable. The physical accommodations are in order: play structures for the kids, with benches at the side for parents; blacktop surfaces and hoops for the basketballers; lawn with edge boards for the bocci players.

5.16 Scheme A treats only the overt activities; Scheme B considers the sociopsychological agenda as well.

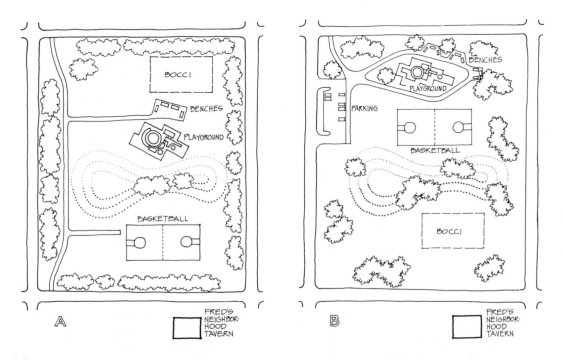

Area organization appears equally adept. Having nothing in common with the playground, the basketball court has been placed at some distance away and further separated by earth mounds and plantings that prevent a mix of tots and teens. Owing to the tightness of the site, the bocci green has been located in the only other available space. It is near the playground, but happily buffered from the scurrying kids by the parental sitting area. That placement seems enlightened on its own. The sitting space can serve either use area equally well. Moreover, like the tennis-playground setup previously described, parents can watch other action while remaining well within reach of their children. As a final stroke, the site has been edged with attractive plantings to screen off surrounding streets.

A friend of mine once took his lady on a Sunday-morning stroll through a New York City park, stopping along the way to watch a bocci game. As they stopped, so did the game. Nothing was said, but the nonverbal messages were clear enough to distress the couple, and they ceased only when the couple left. Why? Played for keeps there, bocci was not only a game but also a full-blown social ritual. It was for males only, and the mere presence of a woman rubbed against the grain. In that same social tradition, women mind the kids and teen girls are given the explicit task of seeing to the needs of their younger siblings after school. They like boys, of course, but there are social stigmas on blatant associations without parental consent. The teen boys, however, are not burdened by such societal strictures. They run in male packs, and they take advantage of every opportunity to show off in front of the girls. If you can, cast your personal biases aside so that you may consider this analysis without editorializing over it. If you can't, we will deal with that shortly.

Note Fig. 5.16B. Here physical accommodation and use area organization criteria have been met, but by responding to the sociopsychological agenda, we have come up with a different plan. The bocci green has been slotted in the more isolated spot and thereby removed from the playground, where the women are most likely to be. Furthermore, the peripheral screening around the bocci green has been loosened so that the area ties in with the neighborhood tavern, the social hub for the older males, who play the game. The basketball court, prime territory for teen males showing off, is now within view of the sitting area on the far side of the playground where teen girls are likely to congregate. Minding their siblings at play legitimizes the young females' presence near where the boys hang out. They can retain an appropriate social distance by entering via the far access path and remaining in the sitting space. Yet they can still "casually" run into the guys if they choose, for the other access path leads by the basketball court. A parking lot has been added in violation of the planning convention that one designs a neighborhood park strictly as a walk-to place. The

users here, however, are primarily teens—teens with autos. These autos are equipped like rolling living rooms, complete with shag carpets and quadrophonic sound. Cruising is the name, peer view the game. In keeping with these teens' socio-psychological predispositions, one with confidence can bet that this place will be their social hub.

About Consequences. I anticipate some strong reaction, but less perhaps to the plan than to aspects of the social scenario which the design proposes to support. Not the least of objections may be to the picture drawn of teenagers doing nothing terribly constructive, simply hanging around. If so, I find that a curious indictment. "Hanging out," is and always has been a primary adolescent activity for sorting out identity in the company of peers. Yet while accommodating this need for teens is largely ignored in site development programs, providing places for older adults to hang out is routine. An immediate case: were eyebrows raised as high when I addressed the bocci-tavern side of the park?

Hanging out in peer groups is a most ordinary tendency that knows no age bounds. Built upon shared interests, hanging out together is institutionalized in fraternities, sororities, Elks, Moose, Masons, and all sorts of clubs. The tendency also gets satisfied in quasi-structured fashion when middle-class housewives, for instance, gather around bridge tables weekly or koffee klatch from house to house. True, teens are more boisterous than most and their behaviors are often judged outrageous by certain standards. But really, are those behaviors as malicious and their perpetrators as "delinquent" as a common perception would have them be? Or are they simply foreign to the beholder's own mode of conduct when he or she hangs out?

Ultimately, those are the kinds of questions which must be answered by designers when confronted with the predispositions of others. Consistent with Dewey's emphasis on the weighing of consequences, the idea is not merely to "give them what they want." Like everyone else, designers have consciences, and it should not be expected they would want to be party to advancing truly destructive acts. Indeed, it is to their credit to refuse flatly to oblige a predisposition that is clearly perverted, demeaning to spirit, or ruinous to health. There should be little argument, for instance, in favor of setting aside glue-sniffing cubicles around grade-school playgrounds or providing supportive environments for flashers, no matter how pervasive those behaviors might be.

The big problem for designers lies with issues that cannot be readily objectified and the way that such issues leave one vulnerable to making biased value judgments. Upon what basis, for example, does a designer conclude that winos and pensioners ought to transcend their animosities and therefore redesigns an

5.17 Hanging out with peers is something every age group does.

urban California park to bring them together? Why might you decide that communing with nature is more valuable than communing with fellow campers? Can you rightfully hinder the Peruvian host-guest ritual upon reasoning that the game is silly and people ought to be up front when interacting with friends? Do you personally oppose the chauvinistic family model of a few paragraphs ago, and would you refuse to design a place reinforcing its patterns? Do you tag ogling as offensively sexist and therefore reject much of what we've written about seeing and being seen? How do you react to gay lifestyles, nude sunbathing, or gangs securing turf?

Clearly, decisions to encourage or discourage such predispositions are up to each individual. I know of no guaranteed recipes you can use. But to ensure that you do not engage in bias intervention when creating a design, you might try approaching each case by considering *your behaviors as being different from others'* rather than the reverse, which is the more common way. Then go from there.

Inviting Change. Beyond a refusal to encourage blatantly ruinous behaviors, there may be other valid reasons for denying users their behavioral preferences. These might include conditions where trading off old ways is essential for accommodating more pressing needs. Such could have been the case if barricading the cane-pole fishermen's stream had been aimed at preventing tots from tumbling in. Consider, though, that every time a designer denies the execution of a familiar routine either by failing to provide supporting facilities or by throwing up obstacles, he is, in effect, issuing an invitation for behavioral change. The question then becomes one of determining the effectiveness of a design for actually bringing a modification about. In that behavioral formation comes from a multideterminant process, so too does behavioral alteration. Physical design cannot manage the job alone.

In *Planning for People*, architect Maurice Broady refers us to the impotency of design as a unilateral agent with his story of a British university plan meant to enhance communications between students and faculty. An inviting coffee lounge with soft chairs and thick carpets was installed between student and staff common rooms. Nobody used it. It would not have worked, Broady submits, "without supporting social and possibly administrative arrangements." For it "is quite unrealistic to suppose that the provision of a coffee lounge could change a pattern of social segregation which rests upon substantial differences of function and responsibility, not to mention age and status, and which the whole pattern of academic organization tends to emphasize."

When change is imagined to be in order, physical design must be part of an overall strategy if it is to be effective. And in

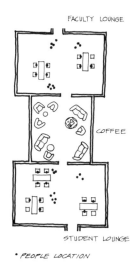

FACULTY LOUNGE

COFFEE

STUDENT LOUNGE

• PEOPLE LOCATION

5.18 Counting on physical design alone to do the job, this plan failed to get the students and faculty to change their aversion to social mingling.

the most successful packages, we will probably find that a trade-off was made whereby the loss represented by retiring a predisposition was offset by some other *tangible gain*. The gain should be immediately apparent. As has been experienced with many envrionmental issues, strategies built upon distant, theoretical, or probable profit are unlikely to wash. Even when survival is conceptualized to be at stake, as it was in the early stages of the energy problem, the major run to insulate homes did not occur until a tax write-off was guaranteed.

On a matter close to the heart of park authorities, a while back government researchers confronted the problem of litter and experimented with ways of getting folks to stop being slobs and at least pick the stuff up. They selected a movie theater for a trial run, preceding the feature with an antilittering short appealing to pride and citizenship. Not a dent in the residue of popcorn boxes and candy wrappers on the floor was made. Considering that some might not have been paying attention, the researchers then distributed handbills describing the virtue of neatness. As you might suspect, these ended up on the floor with the resident mess. Next they handed out trash bags. Minimal results. Only when it was announced that premiums like munchies and passes would be given out to those turning in a full bag did the mess begin to get picked up. Indeed, they succeeded too well. Some patrons began bringing their own trash bags, only to be sorely put out to find that the experiment had ended. Turning their attention to a campground, the researchers gave trash bags to each entering family and offered as a reward a junior forest ranger patch for every kid who returned with a bulging sack. It worked.

Although many might deem it philosophically debasing to consider, it remains a truism that the dollar is among the most effective incentives going. Recently, a West Coast newspaper reported that vandalism had robbed a local junior high budget of $20,000 for repairs. Officials made a pact with the students that if they would police themselves, a healthy percentage of the repair bill saved would go into a student activity fund. Within a year, that fund had gained $8,000. As the president of the student government pronounced: "The money said it all. That's what did it."

The lowering of social sanctions has proved to be another mighty force in effecting behavioral change. In a midwestern black community, a recreation building suffered the insult of chronic, rotten-mouth graffiti on its most visible wall. An artist was brought in to paint a mural depicting the black experience in America. It was labeled the "Wall of Respect." Nobody, read *nobody*, dared think about besmirching that facade after that.

As for the role of physical design in a strategy to alter predispositions, I see it once more acting effectively as a servant, this time as a *servant to the more potent agents of change*. To illustrate

5.19 Behavioral change may be brought about by the introduction of tangible inducements. Vandalism may be brought to bay, for instance, by the promise of cash incentives or the implicit threat of social sanctions.

that idea in a particular social context: the mere availability of close-together and facing benches did not move Anwar Sadat and Menachem Begin to talk to each other. But when more potent forces led them to negotiate, face-to-face benching undoubtedly facilitated that behavior, whereas back-to-back and far-apart arrangements would have hindered their action.

A Regard for the Here and Now. Behavioral predispositions provide the common ground from which designers and users (and, indeed, behavioral scientists) can work to mend the divisions between them. A sensitive regard for predispositions is pertinent even where designers introduce new opportunities in the interest of expanding user horizons or otherwise enriching lives. A balancing out with the old may be in order. New overt activities may be more readily accepted, for instance, if the existing sociopsychological agenda remains supported by the design.

In that sense, attending to predispositions is to design with one slice of time in mind. If that seems unduly restrictive to creativity, take into account that the only futuristic-sounding

5.20 The physical accommodations facilitated the behavior, but only after more potent forces prompted these erstwhile enemies to negotiate.

87

proposals that anyone takes seriously are reactions to problems which bubble about in the here and now. The present is the common reference point. I also think that the idea of designing environments which are adaptable to future needs is much overrated. As our plaza discussion demonstrated (religious processions once, flea markets now), design forms and layouts couched in the present may adapt themselves nicely to the future. I find it especially strange, if not disconcerting, that most people who speak about making projects flexible for the future stop short of forecasting what those distant needs might be. Without something known to guide the thinking, one may come up with works so off the mark both present and future that nobody at any point in time is well served.

Of course, user dispositions might change so completely over the years that a designed environment loses all of its utility. The solution for that problem is obvious. When a place runs its course, it must be redesigned with a hefty regard to the prevailing here and now.

Risks of Ignoring Behavioral Predispositions

The assignment of design to a servant's role may repel many who imagine themselves as leaders, not followers, in the struggle to improve the quality of life. I would ascribe their pique less to substance than to the way they have elected to interpret certain words. For my part, "servant" may be an unfortunate choice of terms to begin with because of the abject specter it can dredge up. Yet, once returned to the context in which it has been developed, the idea of supporting ("serving") predispositions connotes leadership in bringing about user satisfactions, which, by ordinary measures, is an ennobling goal. If that's not enough, be reminded that they award Oscars for supporting performances, too.

Stress. As for the brand of satisfaction involved, Constance Perin offers a theory of "competence." In noting how one's everyday anxieties may lessen when one is "surrounded with things one is sure of: the customs of the group, the familiar place and the beaten path," she attributes great comfort to being able to understand, if not gainfully to handle, a situation and thus to feel in control of one's life. In contrast, confrontations with the unfamiliar can generate spasms of confusion and helplessness. They court the possibility of failure and can exact a psychic tax even when the brain clears one of fault. That tax we often call stress.

That's part of life, you say. True. It is also the stuff out of which evolution proceeds. Calling for human adaptations, stress may produce physiological responses, that, over an extreme length of time, could terminate in an involuntary alteration of genetic compositions. Thus, the fittest survive. Constant confrontations with smog, for example, could lead to the evolution of resistant lung systems. The process toward such an eventuality is not taken lightly, however. A lot of people are going to die from emphysema first. More closely associated with behaviorally incompatible design than physiological responses are responses to stress in the social milieu. Touching attitudes and values, the workings of social stress are much more visible than what goes on in physiological scenarios. Moreover, adaptations in its wake are voluntary and may be evidenced over a shorter period of time. Perhaps because calls for social adaptations are so familiar, and because responses lie well within an individual's control, an ordinary inclination is to regard socially stressful conditions solely in virtuous terms. We hear that stress keeps the intellect alert and the adrenalin pumping. It creates jolts that cause reflections upon preconceptions and produces livening tensions that dislodge the human spirit from stultifying ruts. It contributes to personal and societal growth. In the least, it makes life interesting.

Although stress may do all of those things, and despite testimonials from individuals alleging that they "work best under stress," it must also be received as less than exclusively your fun-type thing. The eminent psychiatrist, Roy W. Menninger, cites depression as the most common tax paid for the absorption of stress in generous amounts. Stress has also been declared responsible for ulcers and chronic high blood pressure. It has been hypothesized as triggering the release of fats which the body is unable to metabolize and therefore as advancing susceptibility to coronary attacks. In addition, Menninger estimates that up to 70 percent of such minor ailments as colds, backaches, insomnia, and fatigue are "psychosomatic reactions to problems of living." Moreover, stress-related depressions have been found to invoke such loss of will that patients' recovery from physical illnesses have been jeopardized. In contrast, happier prognoses are possible when patients are in a state of psychological ease. Collecting it all together, Menninger thinks that the increases he notes in serious illnesses are partially due to stress caused by the rapidly changing lifestyles Americans face. This only echoes the earlier contention of *Future Shock* author Alvin Toffler, who judged many contemporary neuroses and irrationalities as fallout reactions to the rate of change being forced upon the population. Biologist René Dubos has expressed similarly that demands to change are proceeding so rapidly that not only social but physiological adaptive processes cannot keep pace.

Evidence has it that human beings are the most adaptable animals and that, upon call, some will convert their ways with only fleeting disorientation. Yet others may adapt only in slow

5.21 Confrontations with the unfamiliar may generate stress.

motion and therefore pay a substantial price. Some, as Gans exemplified in the depressed Boston West Enders, may never make the transformation at all. This is not to suggest that humans are completely incapable of adjusting to a foreign environment. It asks for a recognition that adaptive mechanisms do not function painlessly in many cases and in some instances, may cause irreparable damage. My purpose is simply to caution against indiscriminate tinkering with the familiar surroundings of others.

We have stated, and I hope clearly, that there can be pragmatic as well as energizing reasons for encouraging the sacrifice of habits. But if not, a designer should serve the predispositions at hand. The upshot would not be to eliminate stress from life. That would involve an illogical assumption. Nor would it touch another's ability to handle a stressful situation, which actually determines its positive or negative effect. But as with relationships in which one party avoids placing arbitrary demands upon the other, serving predispositions can ease the pressure by removing some unnecessary confrontations with choice. To be oblivious to user predispositions in design risks the exactment of an avoidable and needless tax.

Risking Dollars by Not Making Sense.   Thus far, the focus has been upon bringing satisfactions to users and, conversely, on how the slighting of predispositions risks generating discomforts among them in varying degrees. Much of the argument has been built upon intangibles. The word "satisfaction" itself, for instance, is difficult to define, much less to measure and therefore may not move those who are predisposed (if you will) to deal in concrete terms. Okay. For those hard-nosed types, let's strike close to home by turning to designers' satisfactions and examining the risks they take when behavioral predispositions are ignored. The "concrete" side has its intangible side too: conceivably, designers accrue satisfactions upon experiencing a job well done and are subject to discomforts, if not gut-wrenching stress, when confronted by projects that do not work. But more importantly, a poorly conceived environment represents a wasteful expenditure of time and money. You can't get more concrete than that.

Previous examples have amply demonstrated the possible effects of *nonuse*. Too often dollars have been spent for the design and construction of facilities that end up lying vacant or opportunities have not been seized to provide amenities where they will do the most good. Ill consideration of user predispositions also risks *misuse*, a term usually defined as mischievous, destructive, or in some sense improper utilization of a facility. Yet even where destruction is involved, it might also be interpreted as resulting from use contrary to the designer's expectations. To clear that one up, we must ask where the impropriety actualy lies: with the user's action or with what the designer has provided in the place?

To accommodate in design and correctly to anticipate user inclinations diminish the need for external management once the design is built. Maintenance costs, for instance, can be held to a manageable level, whereas constant (and usually unbudgeted) repair work may be necessitated by the inability of a facility to withstand the impact of activity which is second nature to the user but has not been acknowledged in design. Expensive maintenance was necessary for all those objects we mentioned which are subject to leaning or sitting upon where people watching occurs. Policing routines to enforce restrictive policies can also be avoided by sensible design. To illustrate, consider a playground fence: it is sure to be climbed on in the course of play. If designed with horizontal slats lightly nailed to posts, it will probably be destroyed. But if made especially sturdy and, better yet, integrated as a link in the system, no signs or supervisors will be needed to ward off the kids. Much less would undue repair work be required to keep it intact.

Attempts to thwart natural inclinations with signage and patrolling reach absurd lengths where behaviors are not only clearly expected but overtly enticed by the design. I recall seeing, for example, a play structure on the order of a Mississippi riverboat which was certain to be swarmed over as ants swarm over a honey pot, for that is consistent with the nature of play. Yet according to decrees laid down on a nearby billboard, in (as one kid put it, "yukky") verse, that kind of play was simply not going to be. "Walking on the catwalk is fine," one line read, but "climbing up the slide decline." Moreover, "the upper deck and building roofs are not for tag or running hoofs. . . ," and it went on like the fine print in an insurance policy. How many kids would respond so exactly? How many would remember? How many can even read?

In that same park I also wondered how many youngsters had their urges to slosh suppressed by the "no wading" admonitions stenciled every twenty feet or so on rocks along the banks

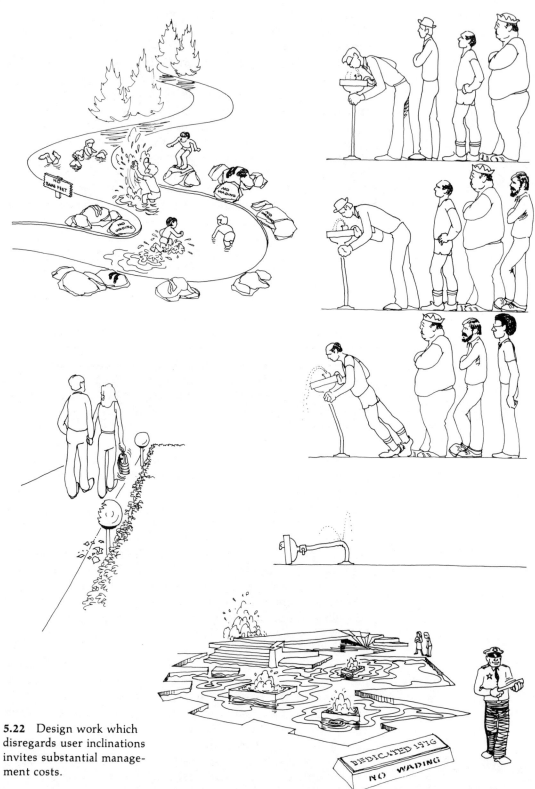

5.22 Design work which disregards user inclinations invites substantial management costs.

5.23 It may be a light fixture, but it looks like a trash can.

5.24 The phony ship's vent is the trash can. Apparently, only its designer understood that.

5.25 Without cues which reinforce its purpose, a feature becomes most vulnerable to various interpretations of its use.

of an artificial stream created as an idealized expression of rural landscape. Not too many, I suspect. The place was brimming with waders, and the rocks bearing the warnings were taken as fine places to stash one's socks and sneakers.

The top award, though, must go to the water complex I once ran across in a West Coast downtown mall that was decidedly designed as a participatory fountain. But rather than permit any participation, the administering agency hired a guard whose only assignment was to chase people away.

There may have been mitigating circumstances in all of these cases. Perhaps the riverboat mock-up was a philanthropic donation, and, even though underdesigned, still had to be moored there in deference to political clout. The stenciled admonitions may have been a response to overreactive legal advice. The waterworks guarding could have been the result of hazardous detailing. Yet, generally speaking, the expensive and questionably effective, prohibitions would not have been necessary if the powers had only followed Rutledge's First Rule for Avoiding Misuse: *If you don't want something to be used in a predictable fashion, don't put it there to begin with.*

Rutledge's Second Rule on the topic states: *If you want something to be used for a particular purpose, cue that purpose as clearly as you can.* Misuse in the sense of actions contrary to planner's intentions can often be traced to an ambiguous, if not totally false, impression a design may give about an object's function. For example, in a park-entry space, I once spied a covey of waste-high light fixtures which appeared similar to institutional waste receptacles. Each was cylindrical, finished in baked white enamel and had a domed top with semicircular openings on two faces. Inside the dome was suspended the bulb. During the daytime, you couldn't see the bulb unless you were a midget or unless you bent down and looked. Most people passing by, being rather tall and inclined to limit their stooping, simply responded to first impressions by flipping banana peels, ice cream wrappers, and other crumpled-up rubbish into the void. Then, as nature would have it, the stuff went on to rot. The opposite process occurred in a waterfront plaza where a designer's penchant for cuteness had moved him to spot mock ship vents about, into which he had inserted trash baskets. It turned out to be an effective disguise. The shrouded baskets were habitually empty, while McDonald's bags and abandoned newspapers decorated the ground.

Hence, be prepared. If something appears to be "X," it may be used for what "X" is usually intended; if it doesn't strike a familiar note, it may not be used at all. If the thing is subject to several interpretations, it may become open season as to its use. I know of a park pavilion, for instance, that was installed over seventy years ago as an axial terminus in celebration of the geometric design which was then the pervasive visual style.

Physical changes over decades have obliterated much of the original setting, and the structure now just floats among walks and lawn. Designers and other students may appreciate the pavilion's presence. In the old style, a feature just had to go there. But others, and in this case the teenagers who have now taken to colonizing the structure, may likely ask: What's it for? In the absence of a clear message, the teens use it like a giant school notebook: the walls are pages for scribbling graffiti, some of which is pretty raw. Let's say, though, that the surroundings were returned to their gardenesque state so as to give an obvious context to the pavilion. Or say we rolled in lunch carts and tables with colorful umbrellas and turned the structure and its environs into an outdoor café. The feasibility of these specific suggestions aside for the moment, regard the general drift. Would there be less inclination to write garbage-mouth messages on the elements of a formal garden or on what is clearly a restaurant wall? Other measures may be called for, as we'll develop shortly. Suffice it to note here that the park agency decided only to sandblast the structure in question. The four-figure expense spiraled down the drain, for the pavilion was retattooed by the end of the following year.

The environment is laced with physical cues about expected behaviors. In that it is not unusual to desire some predictability in life, it may even be said that many people seek such cues continuously and are comforted by their presence. Amos Rapoport suggests that fulfillment of this desire contributes much to the success of many restaurant chains. Come upon the golden arches or an orange tile roof, for example, and without asking, you're immediately informed that all the kids in your car are welcome regardless of their sloppy table manners and that you can invade the place dressed as you are. Spy a Polynesian motif with an attendant at the door, and a different message springs forth. See a clapboard building with a sign saying "Charlie's," and, well, you just don't know.

As noted in our discourse on aesthetic mood messages, behavioral cues must be processed before they take hold. Rapoport says three steps are involved: (1) one must first notice the cue, (2) then be able to understand its meaning, and (3) then agree to act according to its message. Although in general the latter two, and especially the third, are beyond a designer's control, the first step, through the provision of a highly visible statement, lies central to the act of design. It is also the trip step in the system, for if the cue is not noticeable, the other phases will not take place. More importantly, lack of absolute control notwithstanding, the kind of cue which the designer delivers may influence understandability. And repeating the bottom line of the aesthetic analogy, if the cue is aligned with the user's predisposition, the probability of action as the message suggests is advanced.

Managing Graffiti and Similar Assaults. With that reminder in tow, let's return to the pavilion's defacement as a vehicle for exploring further possibilities for neutralizing alleged misuse. First, give an immediate reaction to each of the following, which I've recorded from surfaces viewed during my travel. Imagine that you were my companion, and attempt to respond as if you were there.

Medium	*Message*
1. Professional printing on a commercial billboard.	"Don't Feel Bad. Trickie Dickie Fooled Me To" with the last word misspelled.
2. Commercial billboard on the edge of a town.	"I Have More Faith in This Man Than Any of His Accusers . . . Especially the Press" accompanied by a picture of a then soon-to-resign government official.
3. Professionally painted on an abandoned building.	"Condon For County Clerk"
4. An obviously unauthorized, hand-painted modification, just before the election.	"Condom For County Clerk"
5. Chalk on a sidewalk.	"When Man Wantonly Destroys the Works of Man, He is Called a Vandal. When he Wantonly Destroys the Works of God, He is Called a Sportsman."
6. Brush paint amateurishly applied on a fence outside a school.	"Welcome From the Children of Our School" accompanied by drawings of multiracial children with balloons, butterflies, etc., and signed with teachers' names.
7. Spray paint on another school fence.	"Satan's Angels" accompanied by skull and crossbones.
8. Spray paint on a factory building sign.	"Strike"
9. Spray paint on a university building sign.	"Strike"

10. Brush paint amateurishly applied on an apartment exterior wall.	No words, just a mural of black people raising their fists.
11. Brush paint professionally applied on an office building's exterior wall.	"Welcome to Louisville" folded into a supergraphic, decorative pattern.
12. And using various means, on the walls of our park pavilion, this sampling, with some pseudonyms and euphemisms where discretion demands.	"Dr. Smith Sucks Eggs"; "Go Tigers"; "Marcie Performs a Graphic Routine," accompanied by a telephone number; "Fred Loves Rhonda"; "Jesus Loves Everybody"; "Idi Amino is Bad Acid"; as well as several ungrammatical phrases using your basic four-letter word and references to the elimination function.

Amused? Saddened? Outraged? Smug? Worried? Was your reaction consistent down the list, or did it vary? If the latter, contingent upon what? The degree of property damage is the most common response: temporary chalk is better than permanent paint; an abandoned building more agreeable than an active place; and a legitimized medium is easiest to take. Not legitimate, mind you, but *legitimized* by virtue of some explicitly stated authority like teachers' signatures or the implicit permission the artistic Louisville graphic would seem to have gained. The nature of the message seems important as well, and not just as it might involve foul language, but also as it corresponds to one's point of view. Indeed, the example which generated the most vociferous rage among audiences to whom I have presented this routine was not one of the gamier expressions, but what I originally considered a benign filler, and an erasable one at that: the sidewalk editorial on Man Destroying. It nearly brought to blows a Sierra Clubber and a dues-paying member of the National Rifle Association.

In park design and administration the root issue is the same as in the previous matters of idling and car washing. Should we bother about such activities as valid ways of using leisure time? There is an added vengeance when it comes to graffiti. Most people seem to question its validity on any count. But wait. When perceived as defacing the countryside or tweaking a point of view, a commercial billboard or supergraphic may be just as offensive to some as scatological scribbles are to others—or be positively received, or simply ignored. What binds all these examples together is the presence of a message. Conceptually, then, validity is not an unthinkable characteristic of graffiti. It stands with the rest as communication of a sort.

5.26 To discourage graffiti, try making surfaces super slick.

5.27 Or try discouraging graffiti by getting there first with your own rendition.

For centuries, anthropologists have pursued graffiti in the form of cave hieroglyphics to learn about the past. I have a newspaper clipping which describes how a U.S. Army division went the same route toward decoding the present. Installing blank posters in latrines, the cadre strove to pick up what the troops were thinking. Administrators at my local junior high school have taken a similar tack by posting brown wrapping paper along corridor walls. Granted, park agency people may not have the same yearning for information. But they may be confronted by a strong inclination among their constituency to inform. The tendency to do so surreptitiously would seem ripe in any number of pressure-packed social environments and especially where it is perceived that authorities will penalize those who speak up front: for workers in an autocratically managed factory or office, minorities in a closed political situation, as well as enlisted men in the army or students in school.

When faced with the high probability of graffiti occurring, as the presence of the above ingredients might foretell, the validity issue becomes less a conceptual matter than a struggle over location. To discourage entries where you'd prefer they not happen, you may have to employ a full bag of design tricks. Consider complicating, if not rendering impossible, the task of writing with common implements by roughing up surfaces. Choose brick with extruded mortar joints, exposed aggregate concrete, or patterns with lots of ins and outs, for instance, instead of smooth granite block. Or, conversely, make surfaces super slick. As we suggested with the pavilion, provide cues that will get a contrary reaction. You might even attempt getting there first with your own (presumably more acceptable) graffiti as park officials did with the midwestern recreation building via the black experience mural. But regard as well the additional dimension in that demonstration. Physical design did not carry the burden alone. In fact, design tricks put to discouraging the behavior could turn counterproductive by delivering an irresistible challenge to those prone to impressing their peers by being naughty . . . under favorable odds of not getting caught. In such a case, nothing less than a complete package of design work acting in concert with incentives and sanctions may be needed to get the job done.

To help the discouraging measures succeed, you may also wish to take a note from the army and junior high school authorities by encouraging the behavior where it might cause less damage and even bring some peace to nonparticipants, as legitimization often affords. In fact, if located adroitly, such as in spots where the graffiti-prone subjects normally congregate for other reasons, an alternative resource may absorb the entire demand. As for those potentially offensive statements which are sure to pop up, at least then they might be away from where the overly sensitive linger.

97

5.28 In cases where graffiti scribbling is a certain bet, consider providing an alternative to places which you wish to save.

No one measure or particular combination comes with a guarantee. Each case will have its peculiarities, and what works will be the maneuver that does succeed. Yet I think there is greater promise in these proposals than in sandblasting your surfaces once a year. Especially consider the final suggestion of arranging some compromise with user inclinations that had been previously handled with the same preventative single-mindedness given to beating off a foamy-mouthed dog. Instead, try defusing the problem by providing alternatives for accomplishing the same end. Or, put in the form of Rutledge's Third Rule for Avoiding Misuse; *Never take something away without offering something in return.*

That rule may be generalized to any situation where assaults are foreseeable upon objects which, by their nature, cannot take the beating. Near my house is a grade school for which one winter's window-replacement cost approached the national debt due to the poor marksmanship of kids hurling snowballs at an outside wall. Seeking relief for the wall and windows, the principal subsequently had several large bull's-eye targets hung on an adjacent chain link fence. It was a most noticeable cue. Its meaning was as clear as a physical cue can get. The message responded to a predisposition. It worked.

Who Is the Vandal?   When graffiti defacement and other kinds of property destruction become excessive, it is called vandalism. That labels the behavior clearly as something the bad guys do. As with the softer term, misuse, this term deserves to be examined case by case so that we can determine who the bad guys actually are. Without question, we will find societal misfits who must shoulder the brunt of responsibility for their malicious acts. Aberrantly bent upon trashing a place, they would seem to be utterly immune to discouragement by any of the tactics we have described. Yet I wonder how much malicious destruction might also be nipped by a lessened emphasis on total prohibition of common inclinations and by more resolute attempts to provide alternatives should some place-specific restraints be in order. Consider what sociologist Bernard Berelson and psychologist Gary Steiner warn in *Human Behavior: An Inventory of Scientific Findings.* "When an external barrier stands between a subject and his goal, he normally tries to circumvent, remove or otherwise master it. When the barrier is not mastered and/or the motivation increases in intensity, the resulting frustration of the goal-directed behavior produces a number of less adaptive results." As one of those results, they cite the well-known possibility of the barrier being attacked directly or symbolically through aggression displaced upon innocent bystanders. These may be things as well as people.

Leading from that is the completion of the pavilion saga. Despite the location of the city high school a block away, which

5.29 To bring peace to the building, the targets were installed as an alternative resource for a predictable inclination.

ensured a teen presence, and disregarding that the pavilion was the first landmark met by the students on their most direct route into the park, authorities strove tirelessly to dislodge the teens from that spot. One measure was to barricade permanently the street next to the structure so as to prohibit the teenagers' autos from clustering nearby. At the very same time, a playground complex was constructed for the younger kids. Shortly after its installation, one of the play system's most popular items, a cargo net, was hacked apart in several places, repaired, hacked, repaired, then hacked again. The damage took some doing, for the victim was navy surplus from an aircraft carrier—and that's sturdy stuff. Malicious destruction? Yes. But to what degree was it also displaced aggression brought on by a wholly negative attitude toward the teens and, contrastingly, a blatant favoring of another group? I grant you the most fragile of speculations here. I don't even know who beat up the net, much less if it were a frustrated teen. Yet in light of the Berelson-Steiner position, I am unwilling to let it go at coincidence. That is not for purposes of moralizing or implying fault, but for the pragmatic value of pondering the possibility that the destruction might not have happened at all if the needs of one live and present set of users had been handled in a less disdainful way.

On safer ground is that facet of the Berelson-Steiner quotation which alludes to a human proclivity for circumventing or removing barriers to behavioral execution. While some may strive to adapt themselves to discomforting environments or, falling short of success, suffer its inconvenience passively, part of the quotation suggests some expectancy for the more aggressive reaction of adapting environments—literally rearranging the physical setup to suit oneself. How much of this do we label vandalism?

But who is the vandal when concrete wheel stops are uprooted from a parking lot edge and regrouped in a circle

5.30 Who is the vandal when users adapt the environment to meet their predisposed and highly predictable needs?

nearby as seats to facilitate conversation among regulars in a place? Who is the vandal when a freestanding wall which used to parallel the baseline of a basketball court is dismantled stone by stone by players who had met it once too often while driving for layups? Who is the vandal in a Mexican-American community park when widely scattered picnic tables have their anchor chains smashed off so as to be dragged into mass formation to accommodate extended family outings which remain traditional in that here and now?

Who is the vandal? In these cases it could be said that the designer is. And in that possibility lies the greatest risk of ignoring behavioral predispositions.

Eyeball Calisthenic 5

OBSERVE PEOPLE ENJOYING THEMSELVES IN SHABBY-LOOKING PLACES to discover what qualities may have been rank ordered above those satisfying aesthetic needs. As environmental perceptionist Yi-Fu Tuan suggests, reflect upon common examples of people pleasurefully engaged in environments "that are not aesthetically pleasing, however lax our standards of judgment." For instance, as his crowning example, Tuan cites tailgate parties in parking lots, typically the nadir of unsightly space. Note the attributes of those environments which seem to support the behaviors observed.

PONDER: How might those attributes be incorporated into places designed expressedly for those behaviors in various manners that *also* meet high aesthetic standards.

Eyeball Calisthenic 6

OBSERVE RECURRING BEHAVIORS for possible associations with entrenched styles of life. Describe (at least) one recurring behavior which is a manifestation of *your* lifestyle or the lifestyle of someone else (or group) whom you know well. Reflect upon a private place in which the behavior routinely occurs.

PONDER: What are the attributes of that setting that either hinder or facilitate the execution of the behavior? (Your response may be in degrees of both categories.) If the setting is somewhat deficient in supporting the behavior, suggest how it might be redesigned to bring it into a more responsive state.

REPEAT the exercise for behaviors executed in public places with a special attempt to discern if your manner of conduct in private environments echoes itself in public settings; i.e., do you have tendencies which "follow you around"?

ADAPT the exercise for investigating habits of subjects whom you do not know well.

Eyeball Calisthenic 7

OBSERVE SPONTANEOUS OR SEEMINGLY "PICK-UP" ACTIVITIES to understand how "free-play" space may be typically used. Note activities in places which have few facilities or otherwise give the impression of being designed with no particular use in mind.

PONDER: To what degree do the attributes of those places befit or pose problems for the behaviors observed? Can you translate your findings into design generalizations which maximize options and provide attributes that serve all of them well?

Eyeball Calisthenic 8

OBSERVE FACILITIES BEING USED CONTRARY TO THE DESIGNER'S INTENTIONS to determine if there is something about the design which inadvertently attracted that contrary use. Note settings which have been designed to serve a particular function, yet are being used quite differently.

PONDER: What is your immediate impression of the object's purpose; what does it familiarly bring to mind? List the behaviors that aspects of its appearance or location entice. Which appeal to you? Are you tempted to try it out? Go ahead. How might the facility be redesigned to strengthen its message as to behaviors deemed appropriate by the management?

Eyeball Calisthenic 9

OBSERVE DAMAGED OR MISAPPROPRIATED FACILITIES with an eye to distinguishing between malicious behaviors and adaptations devised by the users to make the facilities more responsive to their behavioral needs. Note defaced, broken, or surreptitiously rearranged facilities and attempt to trace the performances to discrete user groups.

PONDER: Have attempts been made to accommodate the groups' needs elsewhere on the site? If so, what attracted them to another location? As for the facilities themselves, do they appear to have been conceived with behavioral patterns idiosyncratic to the user group in mind? Are those mannerisms readily predictable?

6 Milking Design Relevancy Out of Behavioral Theories

Thus far, we have ranged across the scientific and the experiential, the known and the speculative, patching excerpts from theories, notions, observations, and anecdotes into a point of view. That patchwork approach is necessitated by the fact that behavioral theories are seldom referenced cleanly to physical-design issues, most having been developed with such other purposes as managing personal relationships in mind. In addition, we have gone so far as to suggest design criteria in order to demonstrate the impact of that viewpoint when dealing with some specific behaviors. The state of the art also makes criteria translation an essential initiative for designers, even though it may take them far out on a limb. Don't be misled by Ellis's workup on play. It is an exceptional package. Although, of course, there is no innate prohibition against behavioral scientists proposing design criteria, they appear even more reticent to chance it than most designers.

103

The "So What?" Test

To help nudge utility out of behavioral theories or research findings, ask "SO WHAT?" in respect to physical design—and ask it loudly. You may quickly separate relevant matter from information which is "interesting to know" (in the sense of making one a hit at cocktail parties, but not much else). The "so what?" test can also separate immediately useful material from that which merely promises design utility at some future time.

Crowding theory poses an interesting case on that point. Not too long ago, this theory was thought to have solid footing as a result of John Calhoun's celebrated rat studies in which he proved that at certain levels of population per unit of space massive physical and social deteriorations took place. His findings were applied to us humans, and a correlation between human pathologies and population densities became imagined. Planners began to interject great reaches of open space into urban settings in order to engineer healthy living by cutting down the number of people on a given area of land. Rats will be rats, but the basic assumption connecting human death rates, illness, vandalism, crime, etc. to population density has been demonstrated highly suspect and, the vast majority of researchers would say, totally false.

It is back to the drawing board to reconstruct an operational definition of crowding by examining impacts directly upon people—not rats, nor grasshoppers, nor lemmings as the earlier work had done. Trying to grasp that state of understanding is like grabbing cotton candy. There seems to be a lot of material, but little substance ends up in your hand. Most scientists now regard crowding as a psychological experience associated with space that is brought about by some combination of an individual's motivations, personality, past experiences, and relationship to others present. Reactions to the physical limitations of a place and such environmental stimuli as noise and amount of visual information enter the model as well. Crowding is a subjective event. Upon being exposed to crowding, a person may experience discomfort. But get this: simultaneously, one may experience exhilaration and other gratifications. That gives the event a potentially positive side. A person's crowding discomfort may also be reduced to tolerable levels through the employment of coping mechanisms as with individuals who have devised means for becoming "alone in a crowd." While possible cumulative costs of coping over time are being studied, including the effects upon such pragmatic issues as task performance, no conclusive results are available.

As for the intervention of elements which physical designers manage, alas, environmental stimuli are seen as peripheral matters, and spatial limitation is argued by some to be the least of the factors involved. People things, such as the relative ability to deal with social situations, seem to be the preeminent variables. Periodically, even the word "space" takes on that connotation, as in "I need my space," which means head room in respect to you.

Density remains regarded by its ordinary definition as a count of people per unit of space, but only in reference to a physical condition. No longer are density figures alone used to forecast human survivability, much less any single psychological outcome. Conceivably, a density threshold may be present when a crowding feeling is incurred. Since so much depends upon individual perceptions, one person being "bugged" by the proximity of a few with another regarding the same gathering as sparse, generalizable formulas are supremely difficult to produce. Even rules of thumb have limited design utility, for density operates at various levels: beach populations along highway stretches, for instance, may be somewhat controlled by minimizing parking accommodations. But this solution works only grossly over the entire acreage and does not address microsituations which might crop up were the people to cluster in particular zones. The crowding response might just emanate from that.

At this point in the stream of gathering evidence, the only definite statement that can be made about density is that, alone, it is not enough to trigger a crowding response. That rings a bell. We have a multivariable model in the making that has enticement for designers, for it includes such factors as density that, in some degree, are within their ability to influence. Yet as to the actual impact upon behavior, the thing which the designer does ends up playing, at best, a supporting role. It is once more to speak of design as servant, and, as such, predispositions enter as well. Here it occurs to me that the effects (both positive and negative) of physical factors such as density are dependent upon their relative alignment with specific motivations. This generalization was implicit in our speculations about camping wherein we tied site-distribution ideas to some notion about what the

6.1 A population may be sparse when density is measured across the entire acreage, yet "crowding" may still occur in particular zones.

sociopsychological agenda might be. Happily, crowding is now highly spoken of as having a motivational base. But we must know more about the actual gratifications being sought under the guise of the overt activities which go on in a place before crowding theory can even have broad-brushstroke utility for design.

By revealing reservations about performance, survival, and other far-reaching impacts, the "so what?" test serves to remind us that when dealing with many behavioral matters, designers must gear up to receiving professional satisfactions less from engineering lifelong outcomes than from contributing to momentary comforts. Some may be put off by this additional prospect of diminished role. But, as with the issue of design as servant, I see the potential accomplishment as meaningful indeed. Granted, on the scale of world events, momentary comfort may score out at a minus nine. But in the user's world it may be the whole jackpot at any point in time, and repeated denials of this comfort may be the stuff out of which his deepest dissatisfactions with a place are made.

Anxiety relief is a comfort dimension associated with a number of behavioral theories which, akin to crowding, involve the handling of social situations. Social interaction is especially germane to park design. Recall way back that Hester identified a subject's perception of others as a priority issue in neighborhood parks. I would submit it is a priority issue in many other public spaces. Hester's findings also support common-sense testimony that the perception cuts both ways: people not only have preferences about whom they wish to be with, but about whom they care to be apart from as well. Yet where social interaction becomes approached by designers, togetherness seems to receive all of the play, while apartness remains mainly unrecognized (the California winos and the pensioners), inadvertently traded off in the program (the St. Louis high rise) or opposed as an ignoble want (the San Francisco apartment dwellers and the neighborhood population). The predisposition argument suggests a more positive attitude be given to whichever preference pole exists, and the following works off of that.

Personal Space

6.2 Animals regulate their personal space.

Through the work of anthropologist Edward T. Hall (which he calls the study of "proxemics"), we have the concept that each of us is surrounded by what may be envisioned as an invisible bubble of personal space. The process of avoiding discomforts felt when our "bubble" overlaps that of another regulates the intervals we prefer to maintain when engaging in social transactions.

6.3 People tend to space themselves apart at regular intervals, too.

Originally, the personal-space notion was another extension of animal-behavior studies. Note a line of gulls on a log, or crows perched on a telephone wire. The distances between each are similar, holding true for the initial population as well as when the number of birds diminishes or increases. While, as mentioned, it is hazardous to generalize too quickly from animals to humans, empirical evidence has become ample to indicate the same tendency among people. The phenomenon of interval regulation is readily observable with bus queues, for instance, or when people rap. As to the specific intervals assumed, the space bubble is elastic. It varies first according to the type of transaction taking place among people: compare stoic bus waiters with conversationalists or, more finely tuned yet, those engaged in love-making dialogue versus persons arranging a business deal. The relationship of the subjects also influences the size that the bubble takes: it contracts when close friends are involved; enlarges as familiarizations become reduced to acquaintances, to people just met, and finally to absolute strangers; and becomes especially expansive when the participants are overtaken by perceptions of social class or are culturally suspicious of each other. While spacings seem consistent among those with similar upbringings, learning may produce interval variations between cultures, even when transaction and relationship variables stay the same. This can result in such deliciously ludicrous exercises in spatial adjustment as an American businessman and his Arab counterpart sashaying back and forth in the office, the former seeking to maintain his accustomed apartness, the latter striving to catch up to a point which places them inches away.

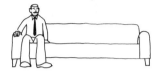

6.4 To overlap another person's personal space bubble is to trigger an anxiety attack.

6.5 When personal space is invaded, people may try to reduce their anxieties by tuning out others by riveting their attention on handy props.

6.6 Observe people sitting on park benches, and note their tendency to assume intervals beyond those required simply to accommodate their physical bulk.

The idea of interval regulation by personal space bubbles may answer why the living room couch is the most underutilized piece of furniture in the house. Ordinarily long enough to accommodate three or four people in an upright position, it seldom attracts more than one or two. During your next dull party or visit to the doctor's office, plunk down close to a loner on a couch. Or if there are two people, plunk down right between them. Since you're in on the experiment, you'll probably mask your anxieties, but see if you feel any nevertheless. As for the "innocents," and especially if they don't know you, do they automatically recoil: fidget, fold legs away from you, pivot askew, stiffen backsides, or go from an easy demeanor to staring catatonically ahead? Do they suddenly become busy: reorganize coffee table knickknacks, leaf through a magazine, pick lint from their trousers, investigate their fingernails as if discovering them for the first time?

To the researcher, these are nonverbal distress signs signaling a bubble invasion, their point of occurrence and relative intensity being the basis for measuring the limits of the otherwise invisible space. To the discomforted person, they are coping mechanisms tripped to take an edge off the anxious feelings by rendering the invader perceptually nonexistent, to tune him out, as one might say. Props that give one the appearance of being rightfully busy are particularly useful. Some well-organized folks even have them at the ready when expecting encroachments. The crossword puzzle section of a newspaper, for instance, serves nicely when one is aboard a rush-hour bus. Other tuning-out props may be simply availed by happenstance: people may watch floor numbers flick by in an uncomfortably shared elevator, or, in the fashion of a literary scholar, they may study graffiti above the urinal when forced next to others in a public john. In light of all this, I wonder if purists miss out on providing a potentially comforting resource by opposing advertising and other forms of posted material in the waiting spaces they design. At any rate, when coping strategies fail to stem anxieties adequately, the ultimate response among passive souls is flight. More aggressive individuals, however, may react to the cause of discomfort with frowns or stares, a colorful phrase, or occasionally even physical assault. For the purpose of defending personal space, the latter is not usually intended to render damage, but more to forward an offhanded message, much like delivering a bump with a bundle of books.

Coping, flight, and aggression, though, are all compensation seekings for an undesired condition. The first-order striving is to place oneself at a comfortable range. Public bench sitting, like couch sitting, demonstrates this preference well. Building upon Hall's foundation in *Personal Space: The Behavioral Basis of Design*, Robert Sommer offers many examples, among them a twelve-foot bench at a bus stop which rarely saw more

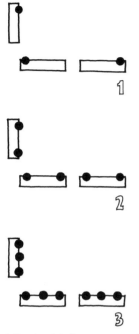

6.7 At this bus stop with six-foot benches, we observed a sequencing trend: first to occupy a vacant bench (1); then to sit with a seat space in between (2); and *only after those options were exhausted* to fill in the gaps (3).

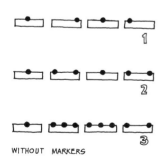

WITHOUT MARKERS

WITH MARKERS

than three users at any one time. If the first to arrive sat at one end, the second usually deposited himself at the other. Although some third arrivals sat down in the middle, almost all coming later preferred the inconvenience of standing about to the discomfort of participating in a spatial invasion. With this, Sommer raises the question of cost effectiveness. The conventional standard for bench design speaks only to the provision of twenty-two inches of width for each rump expected and implies that top dollar is gained when a twelve-foot bench seats six. That arrangement may occur regularly with team members sitting on the sideline of a basketball court. Taking transaction and relationship variables into account, however, how likely is it under other conditions?

At a midwestern bus stop, we witnessed similar sequencing with six-foot slab benches. If they arrived alone, the first customers each unfailingly selected an unoccupied bench. Seconds chose an every-other-seat location. Thirds did fill in the gaps, but *only after the other choices were no longer available*. The difference between this finding and Sommer's may be due to the relationship variable. Although they were nominal strangers, our subjects all were either college students or academic employees, and thus possessed a familiar bond. Downtown, though, where heterogeneity was more pervasive, in shopping centers, and at an Amtrak station, we saw the Sommer finding of gaps and standees repeat itself as a matter of routine.

Across the street from our six-foot bench setting was another bus stop with several eight-foot sitting slabs. Now here, despite user homogeneity, the four-person capacity was rarely reached, and then only when friends came together to sit side by side. As for strangers, the individual bench preference and subsequent end-middle-end pattern ruled, an arrangement which left gaps on either side of the middle person, but neither gap of sufficient width for another to simply sidle into. Consequently, to obtain even his allocated twenty-two inches of rump room, a fourth party would have had to swallow the additional anxiety of asking a stranger to move over. Nobody did. On the next day we watched, we divided each bench into four equal parts with highly visible bands of adhesive tape. By gosh, were the users faithful to those markings! Over an afternoon of heavy-duty bus waiting, only four individuals sat across a tape line; the rest sat smack in between. The tape virtually eliminated people's sitting squarely in the middle of a bench and meant

6.8 At this bus stop with eight-foot benches, we noted sequencing similar to the six-foot bench site (1, 2, and 3, above). Yet the full four-person bench capacity was seldom reached. When we marked off the benches into four divisions (below), sitting smack in the middle was virtually eliminated, and full capacity was often attained.

6.9 People tend to gravitate to corners or to places which otherwise have visible boundary lines.

that four full spaces were nearly always available. And in contrast to the previous day, we saw full capacities realized with some of the benches under conditions of crunch.

Inevitably, some will snort that we manipulated behavior, elitists gleefully imagining a contradiction of anti-physical determinism and hard-core moralists fretting that, like cloaked Transylvanians, we connived to take over someone else's will. Nonsense! The markings did nothing but offer options. To maintain that it was the strips alone that erased the middle sitting would be to believe that the lack of strips was solely responsible for the end-middle-end pattern, too. Since people do have decided preferences when given choices, the productive question is what was the appealing ingredient? What was the predisposition being fed? Recall the item about paranoid patients arranging table service into boundary lines and the ease that square tables brought to their case. Perhaps we are all subject to similar psychoses with those ending up in mental hopsitals differing only through the misfortune of having manifested them in exaggerated ways. Notice how strangers are more inclined to sit next to each other in waiting room bucket seats than on bench planks. Witness as well in public places a decided gravitation to corners: not only the popularity of the ends of linear benches, but wherever the linearity of walls, steps, railings, pool edges, and planters is interrupted by an angular jog. Add it all up and we find one aspect in common—there is a literal demarcation. Could the presence of visible edging be another factor constricting the size of a person's bubble of personal space?

Corners and other jogs not only attract singles, but also pairs predisposed to converse. In one of my favorite watching spots in a shopping center, for instance, couples are magneti-

6.10 Typically, conversationalists assume a kitty-corner orientation toward each other. As in the lower sketch, this fact may even be discerned by noting the placement of items which they leave behind.

6.11 Those engaged in social interaction may snub linear benches for more supportive facilities, even if that means clogging a passage way.

cally drawn to the angle of a large L-shaped bench. The second most popular choice is a combination of the bench end and an abutting wall coping. In this case nothing invisible is involved. The shape of those spots supports the orientation conversationalists prefer. From studying bar and restaurant behavior, Sommer reports this true even when tables intervene. Given options, friendly couples rarely sit next to each other, seldom directly across, but mostly kitty corner. In checking that out for yourself, you do not need to have people present. Just refer to vacant pairs of chairs left in telltale positions following a conversational event. In oft-visited watering holes, also note chairs vacated by small groups. Pursue similar evidence in parks. The juxtaposition patterns will repeat themselves. If movable, benches will have been dragged into clusters. If immobile and strictly linear, benches will most likely have only a couple of occupants with the rest of the group milling about in front. That is not only an uncomfortable way to socialize, typically it ends up clogging a sidewalk passageway. More than once we've observed long benches being snubbed entirely while groups sat or leaned on walls that were nicely juxtaposed and distanced from each other for conversational usage, but meant by the designer only to flank an entry space.

6.12 Alignment jogs support conversational postures.

So What? Regarding design, the question "so what?" is easy to answer. The target of the personal space idea is obviously sitting facilities in public places.

    The best facility allows desirable orientations and distances to be managed easily. The ideal provision would be movable elements that could be arranged by users to satisfy every ad hoc need. Realistically, though, the seating may have to be secured in permanent locations. See Fig. 6.14 which displays the orientation potentials of various shapes. These shapes too ought to be taken into account. As for distances between sitting features when they must be fixed beforehand, a precise accommodation of preferred distances between fixed seats cannot be expected. Common-sense reasoning in the critical areas indicated in each of the arrangement examples in Fig. 6.15 is not, however, too much to ask of a designer.

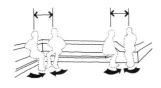

6.13 Desired orientations and distances should be taken into account when designing seating accommodations.

    To guide that reasoning, Hall's description of Interpersonal Distance Zones, which first appeared in *The Silent Language* and which is briefly summarized below, is of some use. Hall cautions that his figures result from sampling middle-class and generally well-educated adults who are mainly natives of the northeastern United States. Hence while the figures may need altering for other user groups, the material does provide us with categories of social transactions and some ballpark ranges which might be judiciously kept in mind.

SELECTED SEAT SHAPES
Showing user orientation limitations and potentials

STRAIGHT SLAB

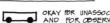

OKAY FOR UNASSOCIATED SINGLES AND FOR OBSERVING AN EVENT DEAD UP FRONT.

DOES ALLOW FOR SWIVELLING INTO CONVERSATIONAL ORIENTATION FOR COUPLES BUT SOME KNEE KNOCKING PROBABLY RESULTS.

POOR FOR GROUP INTER-ACTION. STANDEES OFTEN CLOG PEDESTRIAN PASSAGEWAY.

SINGLE POD

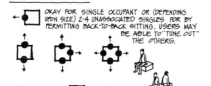

OKAY FOR SINGLE OCCUPANT OR (DEPENDING UPON SIZE) 2-4 UNASSOCIATED SINGLES FOR BY PERMITTING BACK-TO-BACK SITTING, USERS MAY BE ABLE TO "TUNE OUT" THE OTHERS.

POOR FOR COUPLE INTERACTION BECAUSE OF EITHER SIZE LIMITATIONS OR HINDRANCE POSED FOR EASY SWIVELLING; POOREST FOR GROUP INTERACTION.
LONGER UNITS TAKE ON THE CHARACTERISTICS OF STRAIGHT SLABS.

SINGLE JOGS

ANGLE ACCOMMODATES TWO CONVERSATIONALISTS WITHOUT KNEE KNOCKING.

A BIT TRYING FOR THOSE ON THE ENDS, BUT CAN DO FOR INTERACTION AMONG FOUR.

WHILE SEVERAL STILL STANDING, BETTER THAN STRAIGHT SLABS OR PODS FOR SMALL-GROUP INTERACTION ONLY IN THE SENSE THAT (BECAUSE OF LOCATION IN THE ANGLE) STANDEES WILL PROBABLY NOT CLOG A PASSAGEWAY.

MULTI-JOGS

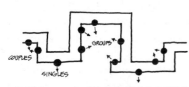

COUPLES

SINGLES

GROUPS

BEST: ACCOMMODATES A VARIETY OF DEMANDS.

CIRCLE

GOOD FOR UNASSOCIATED SINGLES. ARC SETS ADJACENT USERS A BIT ASKEW FROM EACH OTHER, THUS HELPS NORMALIZE "TUNING OUT."

AND ESPECIALLY IF ONE CHOOSES (AS WITH A SINGLE POD) TO GO BACK TO BACK WITH DISTANCE IN BETWEEN.

CONVERSATIONAL ORIENTATION POSSIBLE AMONG COUPLES BUT SINCE THEY MUST SWIVEL AGAINST THE SHAPE, IS MORE DISCOMFORTING THAN STRAIGHT SLAB; POORER YET FOR THIRD PARTY WHO MUST BALANCE ON ONE BUTTOCK TO REMAIN IN THE ACT (THE TIGHTER THE RADIUS, THE GREATER THE PROBLEMS); JUST AS BAD FOR GROUP INTERACTION AS STRAIGHT SLAB.

CURVE

(LIMITED TO CONCAVE OR CONVEX POTENTIALS-LIMITATIONS IF ONLY ONE SIDE CAN BE USED. NOTE POSSIBILITIES, THOUGH, IF SITTING IS ALLOWABLE ON BOTH SIDES AS SHOWN.)

CONVEX SIDE (AS WITH CIRCLES) OKAY FOR UNASSOCIATED SINGLES BUT POSES PROBLEMS FOR CONVERSATIONALISTS.

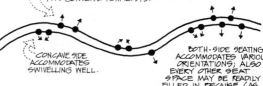

CONCAVE SIDE ACCOMMODATES SWIVELLING WELL.

BOTH-SIDE SEATING ACCOMMODATES VARIOUS ORIENTATIONS; ALSO EVERY OTHER SEAT SPACE MAY BE READILY FILLED IN BECAUSE (AS WITH PODS OR CIRCLES.) "TUNING OUT" POSSIBILITIES ARE ENHANCED.

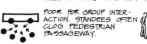

SELECTED SEATING ARRANGEMENTS
Showing some critical distances to be kept in mind (|←——→|)

Where a complexity of use and users is anticipated,
strive to provide great variety in shapes and arrangements.

STRICT LINEARITY
(DUE TO LIMITATIONS POSED FOR CONVERSATIONALISTS, ESPECIALLY
WHEN GATHERED IN SMALL GROUPS, AVOID THIS AS THE
EXCLUSIVE ARRANGEMENT AT ALL COSTS.)

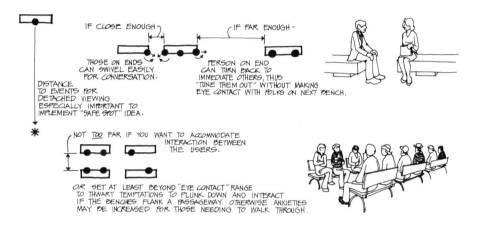

IF CLOSE ENOUGH →
IF FAR ENOUGH →

THOSE ON ENDS
CAN SWIVEL EASILY
FOR CONVERSATION.

PERSON ON END
CAN TURN BACK TO
IMMEDIATE OTHERS, THUS
"TUNE THEM OUT" WITHOUT MAKING
EYE CONTACT WITH FOLKS ON NEXT BENCH.

DISTANCE
TO EVENTS FOR
DETACHED VIEWING
ESPECIALLY IMPORTANT TO
IMPLEMENT "SAFE SPOT" IDEA.

NOT TOO FAR IF YOU WANT TO ACCOMMODATE
INTERACTION BETWEEN
THE USERS.

OR SET AT LEAST BEYOND "EYE CONTACT" RANGE
TO THWART TEMPTATIONS TO PLUNK DOWN AND INTERACT
IF THE BENCHES FLANK A PASSAGEWAY. OTHERWISE ANXIETIES
MAY BE INCREASED FOR THOSE NEEDING TO WALK THROUGH.

RIGHT ANGLES

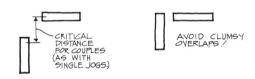

CRITICAL
DISTANCE
FOR COUPLES
(AS WITH
SINGLE JOGS.)

AVOID CLUMSY
OVERLAPS.!

CLUSTERS

VARY AS MUCH AS POSSIBLE TO ACCOMMODATE AS MANY COMBINATIONS OF
DISTANCE-ORIENTATIONS AS SEEM ADVISABLE INCLUDING
SERVICE FOR THE OCCASIONAL LONER.
(THE SAME GOES FOR JOGS IN LINEAR ARRANGEMENTS, CIRCLE CLUSTERS,
AND DETACHED ARCS.)

1. *Intimate distance*, Hall suggests, is 6 to 15 inches, which is agreeable in interactions with a loved one but otherwise unpleasant—in, say, an elevator crush. Its close phase is less than a half foot, but that distance is reserved for comforting acts and physical expressions of love.

2. *Personal distance*, by Hall's figuring, is 1½ to 4 feet, with 1½ to 2 feet being its close phase. The close phase is typically struck among those intensely sharing verbal or silent thoughts. From there to 4 feet, involuntary sensory inputs diminish. Two people can still touch hands, but only if they make the effort to extend their arms. The far phase is therefore a good "no demands" distance for private interactions in that it requires an obvious adjustment if the participants are to intensify the situation, yet still a simple adjustment.

3. *Social distance* measures 4 to 12 feet and is the normal spacing at which most business and social contacts take place. The near phase, up to 7 feet, ordinarily occurs among people who work closely together or are casual acquaintances. As exemplified by conversations on street corners, for instance, it also appears as the most popular distance in public settings. The far phase is for relatively formal transactions.

4. *Public distance* is recorded by Hall as from 12 to 25 feet and is witnessed where high-status persons are involved: bishops enthroned apart from an audience of lessers, judges benched away from attorneys in a courtroom, dais luminaries segregated from ordinary guests in a banquet hall. It is also the distance apparently preferred in the most formal of interchanges, such as lectures, and therefore suggests where the podium ought to be set up relative to the first row of seats.

It would be grand if we could tailor sitting accommodations exactly to each case. We do find that in workplaces, Hall-type measurements have directed the arrangement of office furniture. The task is simplified by the existence of built-in roles and many standard routines. In outdoor areas such as public parks, that kind of predictability is less common. Some general behaviors may still be anticipated and rule-of-thumb applications put into force. Spacings between sitting facilities where conversation is expected should certainly fall between the far phase of the personal distance category and the close social phase. Spacings would be less commodious as they approach the public distance range. On the other hand, public distance is a reasonable range to consider, at least for establishing minimums, when a designer is experimenting with the safe-spot idea and assumes users prefer detachment from others. For years, I've had an abiding curiosity about why blue-collar workmen on my campus habitually spend their break time sitting in one particular spot. The easy answer, and undoubtedly part of the truth, is the opportunity the place affords for watching students sunning and messing around on a large grassy mall in front of the workmen's spot. It should be added now that, while benches on the edge of the mall are regularly colonized by the student population, the seats elected by the workmen are pocketed 17 feet back from where the action begins.

Although a single kind of arrangement may suffice in one-use spots such as bus stops, the more complex a public space in terms of use and users, the greater the need for variety in the orientations and spacings given to seating accommodations. This fact should generate from designers an oath against routine approval of designs in major parks which only line up straight benches every so often along walks. It also suggests some re-thinking be given to the unyielding linearity that often charac-terizes walls, planter copings and other features which might be expected to double as seats. Better to reserve accolades for such marvelous handlings as shown at the bottom of Fig. 6.15. Only one of many seating possibilities well integrated into the visual scheme of a West Coast park it is a water feature with concrete pods distributed around its base. The pods are clustered vari-ously so as to present numerous options for small-size groups while isolated pods serve loners nicely here and there. During peak use time, the clusters are flooded with brown-bag lunchers. Then, as well as when lesser numbers are present, or indeed when nobody is actually sitting on its elements, it also functions as a sculptural centerpiece.

Territoriality

The idea of territoriality is similar to personal space in that both are concerned with spaces that encompass behaviors and reac-tions to invasions of the space. But whereas personal space is portable and changes size according to conditions, territoriality involves a fixed geographical place and a perceived proprietary right to its use. Furthermore, reactions to invasion are less for signaling or compensating for discomforts than for driving off the invaders. Therein lies the key to territorial behavior: it is expressed as a willingness to defend one's space and runs the gamut from grimaces and other nonverbal actions to offhanded verbal and physical messages to actual abuse of a violent sort. Indeed, some cite territorial behavior as a primary means for releasing pent-up aggressions among humans. The original no-tion, however, come from studies of lower animals which mark off and protect their mating, feeding, and nesting spaces. The usual controversy about the notion's extending to the human condition notwithstanding, and the aggression-rite remaining an open question, similar tendencies are commonly observable among people. Habitual gravitations to favored places are well

6.16 Some people aggres-sively display resentment when "their" place is invaded by others.

known, for instance, along with displays of resentment when people find them occupied by others. Archie Bunker illustrates this well when he discovers Meathead in his chair, a display which I have come to regard as no mere fictional exaggeration since witnessing two grizzled codgers come to blows over one's usurpation of the other's usual seat in a West Coast city park.

So what? For environmental design, "so what?" is also a relatively easy question to answer because the establishment of physical boundary lines is a fundamental act in design. Considerable play has been given the matter in housing design, notably in multifamily layouts where, it has been suggested, livability is highly dependent upon the residents being able to identify geography as exclusively their own. That need was the gist of the Cooper finding, which traced satisfactions to the existence of fenced-off space for each row-house unit. Note, though, that the fences served as more than screening elements. As could also be true for judiciously placed walks, walls, grade changes (or as we saw, even with tape strips on a bench), the fences were demarcation lines or environmental cues indicating ownership limits. The absence of markers to subdivide grounds adjacent to rental units has been known to foster a reticence about personalizing the land, while the presence of markers—however slight and unintentional—has been shown actually to encourage proprietary activity in a place. In his study of a Massachusetts housing complex, for example, sociologist John Zeisel discovered that this marking could exist on even the smallest order of a building indentation. Where indentations occurred, personal flower gardens were quite common. In contrast, they were usually absent where long unbroken stretches of lawn or pavement reigned and where the building facades were insufferably flush.

Where identity needs are not at issue, there remain additional and pragmatic advantages to marking off land associated with rental units—as in public housing where authorities stipulate resident responsibility for lawn mowing and general upkeep for each dwelling. Where dimensional cues do not mark the extent of that responsibility, local histories are full of neighbor arguments, some pretty violent, over who tidies up where. In many instances, little maintenance gets performed at all, for it is not too difficult to duck the assignment when ambiguity in the landscape creates ambiguity over whom the guilty party is. When clear lines attach land parcels to specific units, the slobs are quickly distinguished from the scrupulous, and it becomes simple to tack fines onto rent bills to advance the probability that the job will get done.

Nowhere, though, has the territorial notion been more profitably employed in multifamily housing environments than through architect Oscar Newman's conception of *defensible space*,

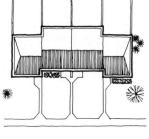

1

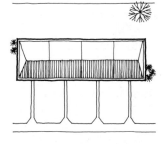

2

6.17 A host of problems can be alleviated if designers mark off grounds adjacent to rental units (1), in contrast to layouts where territorial limits are unclear (2).

which he offers in a book of the same name as a means for preventing crime. Newman's strategy was to increase tenant influence over such typically owner-ambiguous spaces as hallways, lobbies, and grounds by measures that encouraged the adoption of proprietary attitudes and increased surveillance opportunities. These were supported by specific recommendations as to locating windows for resident monitoring of comings and goings. The key was in the implementation of a layout model which used plantings, fencing, and building facades (or for interiors, walls, railings, counters, etc.) to subdivide the environment into a hierarchy of clearly visible zones. This plan stood in contrast to plans which offered indistinct transitions between apartments and the common domain. By engendering discomforts among those who had no business in a particular zone, environmental cues about the relative "privateness" of a space would deter both capricious and sinister intruders. In the least, they promised to cut down numbers in each spatial unit to the point of making strangers easy to spy. Residents were then expected to behave aggressively defensive by questioning the invader, calling up the management, police, or doing whatever the intruder's size when compared to yours suggested.

From a common-sense stance, the concept is inspirational in its potential for reducing crime. Many wish Newman had left it at that. Unfortunately, in his book he sidetracked discussions of the merits by both overstating the dependence of his thesis on animal theories and by forecasting success in the human realm through what some critics maintain are inconsistent and often contradictory statistics about places where crimes occur. He also generated needless quarrels by his architecturally deterministic posture that design *will prevent* crime rather than that it will simply set up conditions which could lessen the likelihood of crime. Newman disregarded the Rapoport assertion that people must agree to perform consistently with environmental cues in order for the cues to be effective. In begging the designer's lack of command over factors like hard-core culprits who ignore the cues or residents, who fearing reprisals or simply not giving a damn, fail to dial the cops, he fueled that ubiquitous false expectation that physical layout and detailing would do it alone.

To Newman's credit, ensuing applications seem to have borne out many of his conjectures, particularly when the physical determinism bait has been eschewed and his planning recommendations have been folded into a mutually reinforcing package of sanctions, incentives, and cooperative managerial acts. Evidence suggests that at least ownership attitudes have been enhanced in many housing projects designed or rehabilitated à la Newman and that many residents feel more secure. Not the least of their satisfactions have been owed to the side effect that comes from marking off land adjacent to residential units: it gives one a stronger basis for hollering off the neighbor's kids than if there were no ownership clues. As for the actual impact upon crime rates, results have been checkered, especially where social systems are in vicious disarray. Typically, though, we hear that not enough data has been collected to reach a final conclusion. And even with seemingly successful cases, conclusiveness is often confounded by a parallel advancement in crime statistics for adjacent areas suggesting that criminal activities may not have been prevented but displaced upon other victims. That is not a slap against the notion. It only demonstrates the complexity of the problem and shows, once again, that while design can be a contributing force to solutions, it must always be kept in perspective.

Meanwhile, back at the park. The exercise of ownership prerogatives appears logical in home environments, but by definition, nobody would seem to have proprietary claim to any part of a public place. The common assumption follows that territorial behavior in parks is only manifested by turf-seeking gangs. That's only part of the story and not always the case. In his Los Angeles parks report, John Lyle discovered that in one place with a "dog-walking territory" the "people without dogs use other parts of the park." He also found that "different age groups inhabit different, clearly separated areas," a tendency particularly "true of the elderly" and invariably of teenagers who were found "occupying territory they have claimed as their own." Previously, I mentioned the habitual gravitation of workmen on my campus to a certain sitting spot. Nearby, in one corner of a public building veranda, you can always find black students gathered. I can also tell you where elderly Italian men congregate in a well-known San Francisco square and confidently advise you to expect their black counterparts in another location across the way. Thus, it is that some portions of public properties become so frequently used by discrete user groups that they take on the appearance of being owned, and by "ordinary" populations at that.

6.18 Through repeated use, territorial prerogatives may become assumed in portions of public places.

Such proclivities are most obvious to regulars, many of whom opt to steer clear of spots which others seem to have claimed. That may evolve from nothing more than a reticence to mingle with people lacking something in common with one. Sometimes it stems from well-founded fears, as Lyle relates: "We found that several parks have commonly recognized territories for sex deviates. Neighborhood mothers are aware of them and warn their children not to wander into them." Regardless of the reason, and dictionary definitions notwithstanding, deference toward an area's domination by particular populations often reinforces attitudes of privileged use. Hence what may have begun as a pattern of innocent gravitations may end up as de facto territorializing of the place.

Deference, of course, may be paid grudgingly and the territorial shakedown process tense, especially when open aggression is involved. Randy Hester and I once served a taste of that shakedown process to park directors in a workshop by requiring that they assume user roles in a plaza convenient to

6.19 Basically, a composition of large undifferentiated spaces.

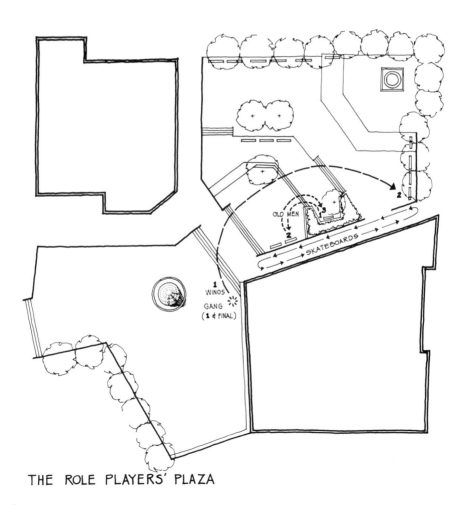

THE ROLE PLAYERS' PLAZA

our conference place. They were to seek out the portion of the plaza which they felt best accommodated the behaviors implied by their roles, then to act those roles out for thirty minutes. See Fig. 6.19. One group assigned as winos chose a corner at the entry to a large artifact-bearing space. Debriefed afterward, they attributed their selection to the prospects it furnished for panhandling tourists. They had settled in for only a few minutes, however, before others playing teen gang members arrived to contend for the spot. They saw in the spot potential for "controlling a major space." Epithets raged, and while all knew it was only acting, both groups found themselves slipping deeply into their roles. The winos, in practical acknowledgment of the gang's dominance, eventually packed off to a faraway corner, trading off their original aspirations for hassle-free respite. Concurrently, a couple designated as elderly men desiring to play cards had gone for a wayside containing one wood-slab bench. Imagining that old men tire easily without back support, they decided to sample a nearby area where the seat slabs had been placed against a wall. This brought them within ear- and eyeshot of the gang–wino tussle and caused them to reflect upon how much control they actually had over this second spot. There were two benches there. Who would appropriate the other? Moreover, there was nothing but air separating their immediate location from that of the other bench. Both were simply on the walkway periphery, in contrast to their initially chosen seat, which stood in an indented space. In addition, as their heads loomed above the wall against which they sat, they began measuring the probability of their hats being snatched by role-playing skateboarders cruising the alley just on the other side. Consequently, they retreated to the original spatial pocket, which was also buffered by plantings from the alleyway. With all due allowances for hypothetical scripting, the exercise worked. An awareness was ingrained that trade-offs had less to do with rights than satisfaction rank ordering and the anxiety-reducing potential of visibly bounded and otherwise defensible space.

Lyle asks for empirical studies to determine "characteristic qualities of setting or situation that can be identified as particular attractors . . . of human use" and a consequent breakdown by user groups. Were these available for cases in which there are social suspicions among the users, we might then be able to load site portions with qualities appealing to each user group. Thus we would hope to cause automatic gravitations and a resulting distribution pattern that minimally inflicted the harassments and anxieties we just described. Each collection of "qualities" would also be encompassed by visible boundary lines. Visible boundary lines could be significant attractors in themselves. Consider how bounded spaces not only appeal to dominantly aggressive groups, but also how they bring a sought-after

6.20 Visible edges contribute to defensible space.

sense of security to others. Visible boundaries may also warn users about the extent of occupied territory. In that sense, the lines are environmental cues which suggest the amount of space one should steer clear of in order to avoid a territorial invasion.

For well-used sites scheduled for design rehabilitation, user groups and the presence of tensions, if any, among them are not overly difficult to discern. (See Suttles, *The Social Order of the Slum*, for example, especially his maps plotting habitual locations of user groups in several parks.) In that the territorial shakedown has probably already occurred, it makes sense to deliver enhancements and otherwise treat the needs of each colony where it presently resides. Such reasoning keyed the planning for a Cambridge, Massachusetts, park as worked out by Randy Hester and his associates in collaboration with elderly users and their on-site nemesis, a gang with the "baddest" reputation in town. Indeed, the gang "made it clear that their hangout area should remain *where it was*, convenient to . . . a street where they worked their cars." The elderly were most interested in "sitting separately from the teenagers." They already did so, but in a spot lacking benches and shade, and therefore had the inconvenience of hauling in lawn chairs in order to sit. Adding to their disgruntlement were criss-crossed walkways that chopped the park up into grassy fragments. Young people ran across the walks from fragment to fragment in the course of their spirited play and, in many instances, literally trampled down the more passive elderly users. It was a teen who finally "suggested that the circulation be rerouted around the edges to create a big grass space in the middle of the park," thus proposing to sweep up the fragments into one clearly defined free play space, "and that another walk-through be provided so that the elderly could avoid the gang hangout." Conflicts were further seen to be alleviated by the visible boundaries which the new

6.21 An example of territorial design responsive to socially suspicious user groups.

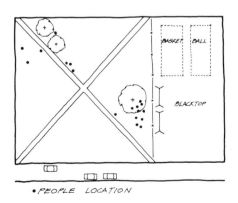

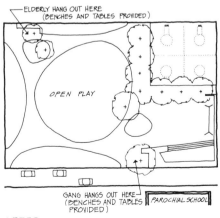

BEFORE

AFTER

THE CAMBRIDGE NEIGHBORHOOD PARK

6.22 A reading of this park's immediate population should have forecast problems with the near siting of the playground.

walkway pattern gave to the teen territory, for no longer would its extent be shrouded in anonymity and its decoding left up to some lucky guess.

Some may find this odious pandering to delinquents and, implicitly, to other asocial groups. Yet, what do you do when their presence is inevitable and you know full well that there are no measures on the horizon strong enough to drive them off? You might wish to ponder the possibility that that which accedes to territorial prerogatives assumed by the asocials may also bring gains for the regular and transient ordinaries who also frequent the place. Hester returned to Cambridge several years after the park's construction. In contrast to the park's predesign displeasures, he found users typically rating the park as "one of their favorite places," and they attributed much of their rating "to the recognition of the various territories and use patterns of the various groups" that was made in the redevelopment plan.

For sites that are being designed from scratch, the park's perimeter condition is a major source for designers to consider when scrambling to imagine its eventual inhabitants and, in some degree, where they might be expected to roost. This consideration calls into question another planning convention. Planners have always theorized parks to have extensive service areas, neighborhood parks, for instance, being said to serve those within a ½ mile ± distance from the park, and all potential users within that range given equal due in the program. Yet in many cases, it has been determined that the most frequent users come from within a block and, in effect, that the park primarily services them. Thus while it might seem unfair, if not politically inexpedient, to state so out loud, it may be realistic upon the weight of presence alone to give perimeter populations a priority edge. Moreover, it should be recognized that for many urban spaces, users will come less directly from home than circuitously from residence to a peripheral enterprise (office, school, shop, etc.) and then into the park. A reading of the perimeter condition may also forecast where territorial enclaves are likely to take root, namely, convenient to an adjacent enterprise. And it is quite likely that the territorial claimants would be those who frequently use that enterprise. I witnessed, for example, in a low-income Pacific Coast neighborhood, how young male adults drank beer, played cards, and boisterously jived around picnic tables next to a playground, while a few mothers guarded their kids some distance away from the playground apparatus. Soon I realized that the tables stood immediately across a narrow street from a pool hall-bar and were being used in a not unusual territorial appropriation as an outdoor extension of the goings on in that place. As happens in so many cases, including our graffiti-laden pavilion within hailing distance of the high school, convenience dictated where to set up

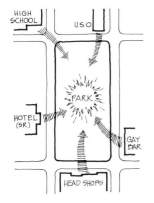

6.23 Would a design comprised of defensible spaces have alleviated some of the anxieties certainly present with this user mix?

camp. In the least, this reading of the perimeter condition should have suggested where not to put the playground pit.

In my recollection, the most astonishing discounting of the perimeter source involved a city-block-size park in a Rocky Mountain community where the thinking not only disdained giving priority consideration to the near populations but managed to deny them any due. That park also demonstrated the conflicts which may be present in a perimeter composition and the classical wishing of those problems away. This site was surrounded by a residence hotel for senior citizens, a high school, a U.S.O. serving a huge infantry base just outside town, a gay bar, and a string of head shops. No one need stretch his imagination to envision contentions among the elderly, teens, GIs, homosexuals, and freaks doing their number in that relatively limited space. As he did in Cambridge, Hester, I suspect, would have brought the combative parties into sessions for some hard-nosed collective bargaining toward clarifying needs and acceptable compromises. Although there appears here such a boggling mix of lifestyles that I find it difficult to imagine a full resolution, I would still suggest that the success, however limited, of any physical plan which might have resulted from this bargaining would have turned on its degree of territorial differentiation. In the least, that would seem more worthy of trial as the pivotal element than anything found in the proposal which the city staff ultimately and unilaterally drew up. It simply prettied up the place with light fixtures, fountains, pavements, plantings, etc. in a turn-of-the-century motif whose nostalgic allusions were held out as able to draw businesspeople, shoppers, and tourists from their usual haunts several blocks away. Even if that goal had been accomplished, did they believe that the peripheral locals would miraculously vaporize? More than likely, confrontations and consternations would have multiplied. I have no ending to this story. The proposal was never implemented; its construction funding fell through. The last that I heard nothing had been done. Just as well.

There is a finish, though, to the development of a West Coast city's Chinatown square. As Hester's Cambridge park represents territorializing responsive to *social suspicions*, this square exemplifies territorial empathy in design based upon the *social customs* of the user population. The major activities in this place are checkers, children's apparatus play, and much, much conversation. That is ordinary enough. However, only the men are seen playing checkers and are surrounded solely by male kibitzers. The Oriental women are wall-to-wall around the playground where the children cavort. A few men may be witnessed accompanying kids in the playground, and occasionally women sit within view of the checker events, but females never invade the male hub. Taking advantage of a grade-change

123

ORIENTAL MEN
PLAY CHECKERS HERE

(NON-ORIENTALS ALSO SIT AT
UPPER LEVEL ENTRANCE
AT THIS END OF PARK)

NON-ORIENTALS
SIT HERE

MEN →

WOMEN

ORIENTAL WOMEN
SIT HERE

THE CHINATOWN SQUARE

6.24 An example of territorial design responsive to the social customs of the user groups.

necessity, the layout is a model of physical subdividing responsive to a predisposed pattern of segregated use. The checker tables are on the upper level in a highly articulated space that is conveniently reached but well removed from the through-traffic flow. The playground is out of sight and earshot on the lower tier. Also below is a space set apart from the playground where (in addition to a space around the upper-level entry farthest from the checker tables) most of the minority non-Orientals sit. If you're not convinced that a use dichotomy was forecast in the program, note the toilet building. It is also a two-story structure, with the men's room reached from the upper level and the women's facility only from below. Large letters spelling "MEN" have been painted on a wall near the upper toilet entrance, and a sign saying "WOMEN" with an arrow points across to a stairway where a similar sign points down. Referring obviously to bathroom entrances, ironically, they also direct you to where each sex predominantly hangs out.

In sum, it ought to be reemphasized that references to gangs, winos, and deviates should not overshadow the fact that suspicions can flare among socially acceptable groups or that they may have customs which may also call for territorial patterning in design. Designers should be especially alert to those possibilities where space is limited, high density expected, and a diverse population anticipated to make habitual use of the site. Under those conditions, strive to forecast preferred locations. Failing that, it is safe to say that a layout comprising many well-defined spaces will turn out to be preferable to undifferentiated open ground as the territorial shakedown process unfolds. Safer yet, spatial differentiation will also serve privacy seekers who may be reasonably counted upon to be present whether territorializing takes place or not. That is the matter to be developed next.

SPATIAL DIFFERENTIATION

WITHOUT   WITH

6.25 Differentiated space not only responds to territorial tendencies, but appeals to privacy needs as well.

Privacy

Before reading on, scribble in the margin your personal definition of "privacy" as it immediately comes to mind.

Psychologist Irwin Altman says privacy is a phenomenon of the mind commonly thought to have several states: anonymity (going unrecognized even though in a crowd); reserve (psychological separation from others by tuning them out); intimacy (ascribed to a couple or small group peeling off from others in order to be alone); and the most extreme condition, solitude (being totally free from the observation of others). He also describes several mechanisms for pulling it off: among them demanding verbally that others retreat (with such benign variations as my parents' lapsing into Lithuanian whenever they didn't want us kids in on their thoughts); nonverbal gesturing such as we have described before—staring, scowling, and shifting about—the latter often referred to as "body language" which communicates desires to associate closely or back off; personal adornments expressing acceptance or rejection of stylistic norms, thus suggesting whom one wishes to be with or exclude; and, finally, in the environmental designer's realm, adjusting the physical surroundings to literally shut off or include others.

As you can see, privacy theory touches all the other interaction concepts we've discussed. States and cues signaling discomforts or strivings are pretty much alike. Indeed, many theorists have it that privacy seeking is at the heart of crowding avoidance, personal space maintenance and territory procurement, further implying a relationship to the latter by citing gravitations of privacy seekers to what we have characterized as defensible space. A major distinction remains. Whereas territoriality is location-specific, with proprietary claims enduring over time, privacy is a more transitory phenomenon. Its seekers are not out to gain lasting domination over space, but simply to take and maintain advantage of a favorable environment wherever and whenever the need wells up.

Privacy has been designated by some theorists as another basic need which bubbles within all human beings. To be able to secure privacy upon call is seen as part of the operation of developing identity and maintaining a positive self-image. In contrast, when one is prevented by external forces from self-managing personal interactions, it is claimed to erode dignity and otherwise demean perceptions of worth.

Now, note your definition of privacy. Is it along the lines of "separation from" or "lack of exposure to" others, or does it turn on such words as "isolation" or "hidden"? If so, you have limited your image to the exclusion of parties and, moreover, implied little concern for how that is to be done. However, if you've used such words as "regulate" or "being able to do what I want when I want," it tilts the emphasis toward process, specifically the exercise of personal command over who has access to you. According to Altman, that's how it should read, for he maintains that privacy has less of a keep-out character than one that stresses control. Its contribution to self-image making is tied to the belief that one is in charge. Furthermore, that command is meant to reign over not only inputs from others but outputs to them as well. This gives privacy a bipolar connotation which can be summed up as allowing one freedom to *open or close* accessibility to self visually, orally, symbolically or physically. The bipolar nature of privacy is most dramatically revealed when both input regulation and output regulation occur simultaneously. At times, a teenager, for instance, will secure himself behind a closed bedroom door, thereby excluding pa-

6.26 The location of this "satellite" bench enabled the users to keep their verbalizations secret while permitting visual access to and from their peers across the way.

rental eyes from, let us say, an independent exploration. Concurrently, he sends rock music blaring through the door at a decibel level approximating an SST as a selective expression of where he's at.

So What? Once more, this question presents no problem for design. First, the idea of control should loosen thinking beyond simply providing impenetrable enclosures when privacy is discerned as a user need. Designers should strive to support exactly what the users wish to control. For instance, while we have said much about teen hanging out from a territorial perspective, it should also be recalled how the layout in Fig. 5.16B gave the boys a splendid opportunity to show off in front of the girls (maximizing control over output) while it easied options for the girls to either eye the guys from a distance or tune them out (self-regulating input) or "casually" run into them if desired (impacting both poles). Additionally, in testimony to the intimacy dimension, it is not unusual to witness periodic gravitations of teen boy-girl couples toward "satellite" places away from main hanging-out spots. In Hester's Cambridge park, for example, as well as with our pavilion of graffiti fame, these satellites were benches located enough out of earshot to keep dialogues secret, yet, in the interest of fostering reputations of being facile with the opposite sex, still well within view of peers.

General design ideas to facilitate privacy satisfactions have already been laid out. At the minimal level of assistance, the corners and jogs recommended to aid conversational interaction have also been mentioned for their edge security. Proximity to a demarcation line assists perceptions of control. Being demarcations in their own right, minor landmarks can serve the same purpose. In the midwestern park example shown in Fig. 2.17, these landmarks turned out to be trees scattered about the lawn at some distance from each other. Note in that figure how the

6.27 Edges, whether they be corners (left) or simply minor landmarks (right), provide a perceived sense of control.

127

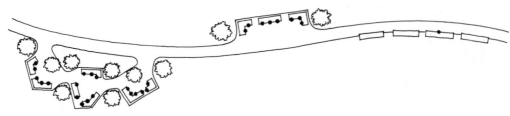

• PEOPLE LOCATION

6.28 In keeping with the notion of control, seating accommodations which are placed in recessed areas are demonstrably more popular than those which merely float along a path.

tree and people patterns coincided but with rare exceptions among those whom we labeled self-contained.

Fuller assistance can be given to privacy seekers by working physical edges into form-distinct compartments, as we described for defensible space. As evidence, in their article incisively titled "The Subtle Differences in Configuration of Small Public Spaces," Joarder and Neill cite the popularity of sitting accommodations placed in recessed areas. Indeed, it was such a space that attracted the card-playing actors in our plaza story. They were not so much interested in owning the location as exploiting its contact-regulating attributes for a time. Adding well-articulated spaces to judicious placement and distancing also caps off the safe-spot idea. For in dealing with the hang-back inhibitions which lie at the heart of that notion, we are actually speaking about privacy control. That perception came together one Sunday morning when I and dozens of students flooded out of a bus into a plaza near downtown St. Paul to the surprise and no little chagrin of its lone occupant, a down-and-outer complete with bottle in brown paper bag. He fled. But he fled not to any old place removed merely by distance, but to a seat in an alcove created by wall jogs at an entry on the other side of the site. It was both a place of defensible character and one which afforded an easy escape route should we migrate too closely his way.

This scenario demonstrates that a motivation putting the privacy need into gear can spring up without warning. It is also fair to generalize that many people come to a park with a privacy quest already in mind. Our role-playing workshop tried to get that across through such assignments as "three salesladies on a break," "a lawyer studying a brief," "two businessmen closing a deal," "a family of tourists sorting out an agenda," etc. None found a satisfying roost, and, moreover, they looked with envy upon our elderly card players for having gotten first to the spot all ended up coveting. Together, this suggests that even though

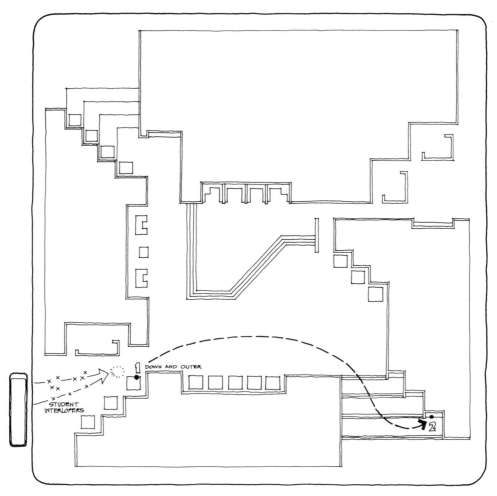

THE ST. PAUL PLAZA

6.29 Basically, a composition of well-differentiated spaces.

privacy seeking is a transitory phenomenon, it, even more so than territorial claiming, is likely to occur under conditions of limited space, high density, and diverse user population. Only its timing may defy prediction.

As with territorial behavior, spatial differentiation is a significant factor in nurturing privacy satisfactions. The more options available, the better the plan. Compare Fig. 6.19, which is the schematic drawn from the site of the workshop experience, with Fig. 6.29, which represents the St. Paul scheme. Note in the former where the card players gravitated. It is that plaza's only well-defined wayside space. It is rather obvious why our privacy seekers groused.

Eyeball Calisthenic 10

OBSERVE PEOPLE IN RELATION TO OTHER PEOPLE to sense affiliation or disassociation preferences. Note individuals, couples, and varying sized gatherings of discrete user groups and their tendencies to locate in conjunction with or apart from others. Notice relative distances and orientations assumed and how eye contact or avoidance may be especially involved.

PONDER: Is there a discernible explanation for the behaviors observed? How are aspects of the physical environment involved through either exploitation of fixed conditions or manipulations by the users themselves?

REPEAT the exercise examining the same groups in other, yet similar settings; repeat it in several different settings. What coincidences and differences occur? Why?

REPEAT the exercise in places devoid of people, yet containing physical evidence of recent attendance. (Before proceeding here, you may wish to familiarize yourself with the discussion of Behavior Traces found subsequently on p. 137.)

Section Three

A People-Watching Prescription

7 | Building Up the Mental Encyclopedia

One school of problem solving says that the subconscious does all the heavy creative work. Although there may be a little more to it than that, no less a master than two-time Nobel laureate, Linus Pauling, once revealed in a television interview that many of his inspirations indeed came from reflecting upon randomly accumulated knowledge, letting it sift itself about until a telling pattern emerged. On the same show, a commercially successful inventor allowed as much, his most recent invention having come together through the process of his lying down on a couch for several days and doing nothing but permitting his subconscious to work over everything it had stored up about physics.

I suspect most designers would have some difficulty convincing their bosses that they should spend a lot of time flopped on a sofa, but even when employed upright, the subconscious remains the instrument of intuition. The more morsels of insight it has on hold, the better its chances for operating effectively when a call from a particular problem arises.

The term "casual" that characterizes the insight-gathering mode we are emphasizing here should not be construed interchangeably with "sloppy," "capricious," or "the lazy man's way,"

133

even though it may lack the methodological rigor of a systematic foray. Its rigor is found in its employment as a habit. That habit involves not only being always on the lookout, but also routinely patching together the happenings of the moment with what one's had occasion to observe before. A telling matter may be missed during a one-shot observation or merely brought lightly into focus. Repetitive witnessing increases the odds of unveiling all as well as it indelibly inscribes phenomena on the mind. As a trade-off for spontaneity, casual observations cannot be expected to produce the documentation that results from the execution of systematic means and must, therefore, be conceded as a lesser strategy for convincing others. But for purposes of building up a subconscious encyclopedia, one has only to convince oneself.

Drawing conclusions from observation is an inferential process, and that holds true no matter how systematically or casually the observations take place. One looks, assumes, and hopes that the speculation made is correct. The speculative nature of observation makes it all the more essential for one to make observation a habit. The more times one experiences a phenomenon, the more confidently are the conclusions drawn. Many specialists would urge, however, that such conclusions should be confirmed through parallel means. Writing in *Unobtrusive Measures*, for example, Eugene Webb and his coauthors suggest that a proposition ought to be tested by three independent processes with each process designed to overcome the imperfections of another. Webb calls this method triangulation.

I also see these processes attending to three insight-producing sources: you, the user, and some neutral party. Observation is your primary tool. It can tell you quickly what the people are doing and where. Observation's primary imperfection, however, is that *why* remains most likely a matter of surmise. Through such commonly used instruments as interviews and questionnaires or such indirect means as brainstorming, gaming, and role playing, with you as the facilitator, the user can bring clarity to that. Users may also tell you what they prefer to do where, but not without some question, for there is often a disparity between what users say and how they actually behave. Observations can sort that out. The neutral component provides information from analogous instances. These include anecdotes which have topical relevance to one's specific case, full-blown studies, and what we have just worked our way through— theories about what's happening out there. The neutral body of information helps greatly in distinguishing idiosyncratic acts and responses from generalizable findings. It can also bring pertinent issues into focus, thereby channeling observation and people-pumping procedures in productive directions.

A watertight conclusion comes when one employs multiple measures addressed to several sources. This admission is to ensure that we understand the limitations of observation as an isolated method and the desirability, if conditions permit, of executing the double checks and gap filling that other processes allow. But we should also recognize its merits. Although observations conducted absent of parallel investigations may generate only speculative findings in certain vital categories, they are at least *founded judgments,* and cumulatively, over time, they produce a sense of real people doing real things in real places. Where that replaces an untested or wholly fanciful image of user behavior in design decision making, it is a quantum leap for the best.

How to Look

To be productive in people watching for design, it is necessary that you observe in a particular—and to some folks—unaccustomed manner. Designers typically see only artifacts and how physical features go together. Social scientists tend to see only people and how they deal with each other. Psychologist Roger Barker asks that we transcend such dichotomizing and look at the whole: people alone or in groups interacting not only with each other, but also with the physical environment in a symbiotic way.

Behavior Setting. The term "behavior setting" was coined by Barker as a unit of analysis for the exploration of that gestalt. Implicit is a breakdown of any general place into spatial subdivisions according to regularly occurring behaviors closely related to the physical characteristics of each space. It thus presents the framework for judging any location by the degree to which its design hinders or facilitates the execution of the behaviors which take place.

Behavior Circuit. Constance Perin provides the term "behavior circuit." It refers to a "stream" of actions involved in carrying out a mission. Whereas a behavior setting is a snipped-off piece of the environment, a circuit may run through several settings and includes the movement pattern in between. Narrowly applied, circuit analyses have proved instrumental in workplaces in revealing the impact of the physical setup upon the efficiency of employee routines. As demonstrated by Taylor and Stone in learning about neighborhood cruising, circuit notations can also have utility in park design even though missions in the business-world sense may not be at stake. In that it involves a charting of happenings along the way as opposed to ordinary traffic studies which simply lay down flow lines, a behavior circuit can reveal where moving about creates conflicts or exploits something unique about a place.

135

7.1 Imagine places as behavior settings: not just a composition of inanimate artifacts (A), nor simply a composite of social happenings (B), but (C) a complex of people and the physical environment intertwined.

Behavior Traces.   Clues to behaviors having previously transpired are called "behavior traces." As illustrated in Fig. 7.2, they are a detective's delight. Traces can give you a picture of a site's history upon those inevitable occasions when you find yourself in a place during low-use or nonuse times. Without the people actually present, speculation may be at its extreme. Yet sometimes—as we suggested when discussing personal space and the telltale orientation of vacant chairs—traces and a bit of common sense may give you all the evidence you need.

Webb et al. classify behavior traces into two types. There are, first, *erosion measures* where the degree of wear on some material is the clue. The most obvious examples are paths worn in the grass—the deeper the ruts, the more preferred the routes.

7.2 Behavior traces offer clues to transpired events.

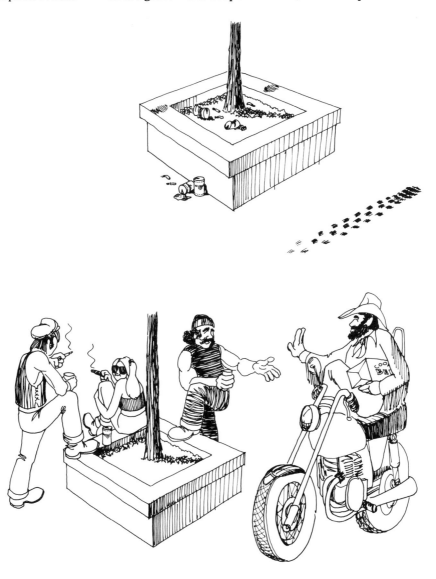

Divots a few feet away from a tree might be heel marks hinting at a popular place where people sit. Bare ground patches behind a bench might indicate that users are orienting themselves in a direction that the designer did not take into account. Conversely, lush green grass under picnic tables or verdent growth in, say, horseshoe pits is pretty good evidence that the facilities are hardly being used at all.

There are also *accretion measures* where the deposit of some material provides the evidence to be assessed. Trolling in garbage cans for discarded invitations and personal effects after wild Washington parties, scandal sheet reporters work this one to the hilt. Less sensational, yet still telling matter may also be available in parks. Fast-food wrappers may suggest lunching as a primary activity and may even suggest where the population comes from. Beer cans under playground structures cue both a social activity and the presence of age groups for which the equipment was unintended. They may lead to questions about what has been done elsewhere to meet various age-group needs. Trash is not the only accretion resource. A resolute reflection upon the pattern of benches left by old men in Sommer's story about the California urban park might have produced a clearer idea of what was going on.

Fortified by the supplementary information that they might send you after, behavior traces can lead directly to design decisions. A beaten-down area on the edge of a lake, for instance, could turn out to be an oft used access point and therefore the logical location for a launching pad if the shoreline is subject to structural rehabilitation. Sometimes erosion and accretion measures combine to draw the picture. Spots where the lawn nap has been continuously flattened and peppered with generations of cigarette butts, for example, are locations to consider installing bench clusters, which would increase their value for the group interactions that the traces imply are taking place.

Role Play to Feel the Environment's Congruence or Its Lack of Fit. While much enlightenment can ensue from detached assessments of behavior settings, involved analyses can deepen the impressions gained. Try putting yourself in the shoes of the users being observed. Actually feel the users' struggle against an unyielding environment or their comfort in a supportive place. We once followed up the claim of a plaza designer that the wall of an elevated level served people desiring to "observe the action below." The wall was of the correct height for sitting. But it did not accommodate a leg drop in the direction of the lower level, only toward the narrow pedestrian channel it lined. Feel the concrete edge dig into the thigh of the typical user, shown in Fig. 7.3, as he contorts himself to check out the activity below. Or, as we observed many standing about to gain

7.3 If the designer were to assume the role of these users, he would find it difficult to claim the creation of a comfortable place.

the best angle, sense the discomfort of sitters having strangers bellying up to their faces as a matter of routine.

Role playing may serve simply to heighten awareness of self-evident issues, but in so doing may ensure that they will not be sloughed off as insignificant. Carrying back the feel of this sitting episode, or as in the L-shaped park example, the nervousness of mothers contemplating a route through the milling teens, does it nag you to the point of wanting to set it straight when contending with a similar case? If not, the only hope left is to sentence you—and deservedly so—to spend sufficient time as those users as might cause you to cry out, "enough!"

By projecting yourself as the user, hidden dimensions of comfort or turmoil might also be discovered. This kind of discovery occurred with our elderly card players in respect to those acting as the gang. Conceded, you may not always be able to identify with the user (or users) because of cultural, age, or lifestyle gaps. But that's a consequential and sometimes the most important lesson. It dramatizes the need for further understanding before you make a decision on the user's behalf.

No less meaningful, where the design is on the mark, role playing in this fashion can also intensify pleasures that radiate from firsthand knowledge of a job well done.

Discipline the Eyes. Systematic observations involve much preplanning spent on the development of notation forms, film logs, and other recording instruments. The spontaneous nature of casual watching precludes such extensive instrumentation. Considering, though, that minds have this thing for wandering, some strategies for forcing one to look and to do so continuously might prove useful, at least in terms of reminding one about the job at hand.

Arming your brain with a list of categories or blanks to fill in, as suggested in the next major segment, can help by way of the focus it brings to the task. Appendix A shows a format for recording that information. I originally conceived this format as a simple field instrument. Yet for the casual watcher, even this has turned out to be a cumbersome tool. Alas, as an associate who tested it out reported: "Having to put all that stuff down while on site gets in the way of the looking." Periodically setting down something on paper remains useful, however, if only for the concentration involved and the effect that it can have on etching events in the mind. A handy instrument for capturing behavioral episodes is the sketchbook that some designers carry around for drawing up physical details that strike their fancy. But the back of a lunch bag will do just as well. A camera can serve the same purpose. Moreover, being less selective of content than sketches, prints or slides provide an information pool for future inspection and latent discovery of insights which may have been missed when the event was live.

Debrief yourself as often as possible. Talking out what you've seen after the fact is another means for ingraining insights firmly, including issues deserving inspection the next time out. Bounce your discoveries off of friends, but if you are worried about their patience running thin, simply sit down and mull them over yourself. Keep your sketchbook wherever you spend idle moments. Rerun your slides, or have conversations with the Appendix A format. Although that format has been disdained as a spontaneous recording tool, it has inadvertently turned out to be nicely suited as a debriefing instrument and especially useful as a sorting-out mechanism when impressions are fresh.

Don't Rattle the Cage. Be an unobtrusive observer lest your subjects abort their normal routines and begin behaving in reaction to you. The more you blend into the scene by dressing or behaving as expected by the users of the place, the better your chances. If you're hopelessly obvious because of, for example, race or age differences, situating yourself fairly far apart from the action may get you by. If a place especially intrigues you, yet you're a blatant foreigner, many visits to the site may eventually stamp you as a regular. From then on, your observations will really be of the action as it is. If you don't have that kind of time or the conditions are particularly inhibiting, you may have to do with a fleeting glance from a moving auto. A quick stop or two to snap a slide probably will not betray your presence to the group. Under most ordinary conditions, an elevated location or one with a wide-angle view is preferable for the multiplicity of episodes which can be witnessed from it. Such a location is especially desirable where the resident behaviors are notably sedentary and where much moving about might bring undue attention to you. If possible, it is also a good idea to log in behavior circuits from a stationary location, following the subject with your eyes instead of your feet. Upon more than one occasion, treading behind a subject has brought on a call for the cops or, more frighteningly, a call for someone's older brother who, with your luck, will probably turn out to be a linebacker for the Chicago Bears.

Cameras may present some special blending-in problems right at the outset if you appear draped with several body cases, lenses, and other equipment reminiscent of a GI storming the Normandy coast. You must also remain alert to the possibility of objections when you point your camera in someone's way (in some tourist traps, objections may be feigned and followed by a demand for dollars), or quite the opposite, to people's acting up like clowns. A bit of inventiveness may be called for at times. I have snapped many a behavioral episode over the shoulders of my kids, and they have yet to catch on why only parts of their bodies appear so frequently in my slides. Upon receiving disparaging glances every time he poised to photograph a couple, one of my colleagues turned his back and shot a large window pane which captured the pair's reflection in the glass. His was a tame problem, however, when compared to the dilemma of another friend who, in striving to understand leisure patterns of a neighborhood, sought to photograph some men rocking on the front porch of a modest house. In the midst of his focusing, a woman raged out of the door, menacing him with a broom. It seemed he had stumbled upon a bordello and a madam who thought it bad form to snapshot her clientele.

What to Look for:
The Consummate Eyeball Calisthenic

When, as a youngster, you first picked up a printed page, the groups of letters in front of you were confounding. Given a few tips, however, as to how those letters went together: eureka! They began to automatically translate into words. Reading was also a self-feeding process: the more you did it, the more quickly the translations came. For some, each reading advanced the appetite for reading more. They became hooked: literary junkies, but also stars. It works the same way with people watching. Upon first glance, the characters may not mean much, but given some starter directives, patterns soon became noticeable, and the more you look, the more automatically you begin to pick them up. As for becoming hooked, with people watching, that usually takes care of itself.

What follows are categories of information you ought to be after. Taken together, they stand as a construct for looking, but only in the sense of getting you started. If, in fleshing out these items, you spy a tempting new direction, pursue it. Spontaneous departures often lead to the greatest rewards.

What. Note the behaviors, what the people are doing. You must first, however, have resolved how precise your notations should be. Simply logging in that the subjects are "playing" may leave too broad an impression. That term could cover a host of possibilities differing in their need for environmental support. But also be wary of breaking your observations down too far into such slivers as "scratching noses," for that passes the point of relevance to design.

With those cautions in mind, we have found that a dual-item system fits most instances well. The first term covers

141

postures or basic modes (standing, sitting, lying, walking, running, etc.); the second phrase holds the key activity (tossing a football, talking, eating, drinking, etc.) and whatever brief elaboration is necessary to characterize the act (drinking . . . wine from a paper bag). A typical reference to *what* might then be: "sitting and watching children play." Sometimes two key activities important to the impression occur simultaneously: "sitting, drinking wine and watching children play." But seldom will more than two of much consequence crop up.

Who.   Note the types of people engaged in the behavior and, if deemed significant, the number of each type involved. Strive to come up with an actual count which will be easy to turn into a general designation if that is all that later pondering requires. If you originally note but "a few," you're in a quandary if exact numbers subsequently loom essential in tying down the case. For the same reason, when massing makes it impossible to count all the heads, a ball-park estimate such as "several dozen" is better than "lots." As for the people-type designation, use whatever label strikes you as apparent, "college students," for example, or "maintenance men." But also be as detailed as your recall can handle, drawing out as many pertinent items as possible from the following list of factors alleged to spawn needs, values, perceptions, and, consequently, many habits common to a group.

1. *Cultural Heritage.* Consider ethnic (Italian) or regional (Midwestern) roots, or religion (Amish Mennonite), or race (Oriental) or whatever subcultural breakdown befits the case. Although for some kinds of studies, each of these items may assume independent status, their lumping under culture puts them all in the context most useful for design. Take race, which may seem the strangest item to be classified here. The fact that a person is Oriental, however, is design-relevant only if, as in our Chinatown-square illustration, that fact can be referenced to behaviors transmitted from one generation of that blood to another or to the response of other subjects in their perceptions of that race.

2. *Social Class.* If you can brush aside its popular misuse as a register for snobbery, consider class distinctions based upon education, employment, and income measures, for social scientists suggest that similarities among those factors produce like attitudes and motivations. There are as many breakdowns as there are social scientists. For our purposes, though, any system of five or six categories will suffice. That numerical area seems to hold the cut point between hair splitting and adequate distinction. The following list offered by William Michelson is typical:

    a. Lower class: low income; often no steady job or one subject to the whims of the employer; little education.

    b. Working class: regular blue-collar employment.

    c. Lower middle class: regular white-collar employment, usually for others; moderate salary at most.

    d. Upper middle class: high amount of education; comfortable salary or fees; sometimes self-employed but skills are transferable regardless.

    e. Upper class: great personal wealth either at present or within the family at some past date; at least moderate education; occupation, if any, is respectable.

3. *Life-Cycle Stage.* This is the way to deal with age. Approximate the raw age, and then quickly fit it into a category best describing a place in life such as: preschooler, teen, elderly, etc. Tag on the family situation if possible: young, married adult, middle-aged divorcee, etc. The idea is that discrete sets of physical and psychological needs correspond with age-family conditions. Thus, child raisers will seek different kinds of environmental support than will single adults or children or middle-aged parents whose kids have left the nest.

    Although life-cycle stage is a handy way to bracket ages, be aware that it is a crude measurement which lacks precise boundaries as to where one plateau ends and another begins. Moreover, as with social-class distinctions, scientists have yet to agree on a single classification system. Categories will differ according to the researcher and the place being researched. Some try to take us from cradle to grave in several big jumps. Heimsath in *Behavioral Architecture* offers a version having seven steps: infancy, childhood, adolescence, courting-mating, reproduction–child care, middle age, and aging maturity. Others give us a finer tuning, but like child psychologists, or, at the other end of the scale, gerontologists, will only address their specialty range. Still others limit their concentration to what interests them. Rhona and Robert Rapoport, for example, leap over the earliest times in writing about *Leisure and the Family Life Cycle* to start off at adolescence. And we all know that in *Passages* Gail Sheehy speaks exclusively about the young- and middle-adult years.

    Considering the variance in available interpretations and the unenviable chore of often having to stitch something together from several sources, we advise that when in doubt, use common terms as seem appropriate to the episode. But also try to develop some consistency in your criteria and terminology over time.

4. *Role.* Despite the pejorative inference that to play a part is to submit to society's preconceived idea of conduct, and thus to forfeit one's personhood, it remains true that people do slip in and out of characters in the course of their daily routines.

Sometimes they play strictly according to their own interpretations. Even if the part has been scripted by society, it may be voluntarily embraced as the way to go.

Much role playing can be distinguished according to occupation of both a salaried sort (business executive, secretary, airline pilot, etc.) and that which may not be done for pay (mother, college student, self-proclaimed evangelist, etc.). Behaviors may then differ according to task performance or someone's idea of the responsibility that any given job entails. Role playing is often a transitory phenomenon, with many individuals changing roles and consequently behaviors at different times: first operating according to a business-executive prescription, for instance, then turning that off to become mother when the occasion demands.

Perceptions of stature accorded an occupation may also influence behavior: a person conducting himself as he imagines a boss must do as opposed to a different set of rules for workers, professors in contrast to students, officers as distinguished from enlisted men, and so it goes. Stature does not always coincide with privilege. The rules being followed, for instance, may constrain activities at higher reaches, as in prohibiting fraternizations between executives and staff members of the opposite sex.

5. *Sex.* As with roles, sex also smacks of manipulating by external preconceptions. Hard as it may be to admit these days, we must still recognize that many people do act voluntarily as "a man should" in contrast to the way "a woman behaves," especially where such dichotomies remain unquestioned in a culture. Similar to the playing out of roles, self-satisfying interpretations of maleness and femaleness may also be in force.

Touching all these bases, a *who* notation might appear as: "Italian, working class, single young adult, union leader, male." More typically, a cut-down version will be the case. First, there are limits to what you can discern through observation. If you are in a neighborhood where all the storefront family names end in long vowels, it may very well be that the locals are Italian. But, on neutral ground, how can you tell? You may also pare the who notation down to only those items which are fundamental to the behaviors being observed. In the Chinatown illustration those factors were heritage (Chinese) and sex (men and women). As for the territorializing going on, social class, life cycle, and role did not appear to count materially. On the other hand, the old men playing cards were responding to behaviors primarily associated with life-cycle stage (teens) and role (gang members). Operationally, there seems to be little reason to note more than that.

Where. Mentally associate the *who* doing *what* with a physical landmark, and briefly characterize the place as: "at the end of a bench," "near a heavily traveled street," "on a grassy mound adjacent to a basketball court" or "around a fountain in a large central space." The characterization need only contain enough information to let you log in the item. Save any finer details until you get to *why*, as we will discuss shortly.

This is the point where a quick sketch can be most useful in seating the thought. It need only be a rough plan of the setting, with the people plotted in as dots. If you have the time, further outline the entire site, and dot in all the users. As is demonstrated by many of our plan-schematic illustrations, such "density diagrams" will give you an overhead glimpse of the place's stress points and sometimes, even better than eye-level scans, may reveal some curious patterns deserving of a closer look. That was the case in a plaza study in which a density diagram sharply brought to our attention a pervasive clustering of users against the wingwalls of the entry stairways and along the railings that bisected the steps which we had ignored.

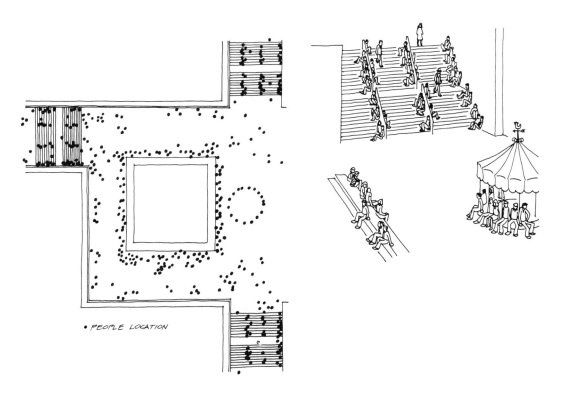

• PEOPLE LOCATION

7.4 A density diagram may reveal unique patterns (left) and prompt a second look (right) to determine their cause.

Revisited through the slides we had pooled, the clusters turned out to be sitters who, by gravitating to edges, cleared pedestrian channels down through the middle portions of the steps. Subsequently, we discovered that this edge gravitation with a resulting maintenance of mid-channels repeated itself with equal regularity among standees on the flat surfaces. It was significant to this study in that we had imagined that the design would not serve its through-traffic function well with all the milling about that was also expected to take place. The density diagram proved us wrong. More important, in reminding us that deJonge, in his article, "Applied Hodology," had long ago discovered a human attraction for edges in parks, it both raised the generalizable prospects of edge gravitation and showed a practical result.

When.   A place may be used differently and by different groups at different times. Behaviors may tip one way during peak use periods and another when the population is light. To discern what is common (or indeed, atypical) in a place, you should therefore tie the time frame down. If you're charting an episode on paper, list the hour, day, and date. As with our suggestion about noting numbers of people, this gives you all the information you need to restate it generally as "weekday," "lunch hour," "morning," "summer," etc., if that subsequently seems sufficient. If you're not keeping a written record, you probably should not burden your subconscious with more than a general term.

Why.   Although there are enough facts present upon most occasions to pin down what, who, where, and when with little dispute, why a behavior setting is selected requires speculation at its utmost when the answer is sought through observation. But that should not deter you from making well-reasoned assumptions, for *why* is the most important item on the people watcher's list. Upon that notation does design relevancy turn.

Paraphrasing Lyle, we must first trust the principle (a speculation in itself) that "settings have characteristic qualities that can be identified as attracting the use that takes place." As we have discussed to a fault, designers are inclined to think first—and often exclusively—of aesthetic amenities as the primary magnet. True, in our role-playing exercise, the elderly card players did tell us that they had initially selected the wayside spot for its shade, human scale, pleasant plantings, etc. Recall, though, that they almost gave it up for a place with fewer amenities but with another feature and that they returned because of other qualities yet. Thus, as we have frequently demonstrated, attributes beyond the aesthetic ruled in "attracting the use that takes place."

Going back now and combing all the examples we have offered, three kinds of potentially decisive attributes which can be inferred through observation fall out.

Taking a note from the card players who were seeking back relief, the first attribute is the prospect a setting has for lending a behavior *physical support*. This is the easiest attribute for you to discern by reflecting upon—as we have also drummed many times—the degree to which specific features facilitate or hinder what you see going on. On the positive side, we have seen how linked systems attract children to play by the manner in which they physically accommodate movement penchants as well as the way their enclosures support sedentary pursuits. Negatively, we recently witnessed the plaza sitters twisting against the grain of the upper-level wall. Why they would suffer that annoyance may be answered by the fact that people can only select from what is available and that those options may not only fall short of ideal, but that the setting observed may be no more than the best of a very bad lot. In the extreme, this making do has been dubbed "the Mt. Everest Condition": people using a place merely because it is there. To aid us in imagining what they might have preferred if another choice were present, note any adaptations taking place. Have the users moved things around, even dismembered some items to make them conform more exactly to their needs? Are they perhaps utilizing facilities in unorthodox fashions? Or, as with the plaza sitters, are they struggling to adapt themselves to make the most of an unresponsive situation? Note also these adaptations going on in generally favorable settings. Adaptations offer clues as to what an ideal might be.

By their reaction to the gang and skateboarders, the card-game role players also suggest that the prospects of *psychological support* may move people to select a place. That thought passes us into the area of the sociopsychological agenda and the most incisive article yet written on the topic in terms of relevance to design. Entitled "Mass Housing: Social Research and Design" by architect Brent Brolin and sociologist John Zeisel, it has been around since 1968. It is about time that it be adopted as a standard way of ferreting out what counts.

Brolin and Zeisel tackled the typical quandary of a literature review: although there are reams of statements about social behavior, even precise descriptions about activities taking place in specific settings, most stop short of providing guidance for design. In other words, they flunk the "so what?" test. Take one of their examples: to be told that adolescents are frequent moviegoers offers nothing about where or how to locate the place. *But* if we knew who else was involved in those episodes, say teens being seen by other young people while concurrently avoiding their elders, we might take it that the theater should

147

be sited within view of teenagers doing other things and not readily visible from activity areas attracting adults.

It then struck the two researchers that useful statements in the social science literature are those which reveal "1. a primary actor and his activity; 2. the significant other in the situation; and 3. the relationship between the primary actor and the significant others. This relationship is the means of including or excluding the significant others from the realm of the primary actor." In their example, Brolin and Zeisel cite the moviegoing teenagers as the actors, the nonmoviegoing teens and adults as the significant others and state that "the relationship in the teenagers' case is visual and auditory connection, and in the adults' case, visual and auditory separation." The theater siting helps break the latter connection while permitting the former to be maintained.

The quandary as well as the solution apply equally to site observation. As Brolin and Zeisel suggest, design-relevant insights are ushered forth by asking not only *"who is doing what"* but also *"including or excluding whom."* Starting with such recent cases as the Chinatown square, Hester's Cambridge park, the elderly card players–teen gang tussle, and the St. Paul derelict-student group confrontation; through the middle with Gans's Levittown and West End comparisons, Alexander's Peruvian host-guest ritual, Broady's British university coffee lounge quandary, Sommer's California park pensioner-and-wino scenario, camping lifestyles, the St. Louis high-rise debacle, the San Francisco housing residents' and neighborhood locals' tiff, Friedberg's plaza's elderly migration, the mothers and the teens in the L-shaped park, parents and children in the Midwestern tennis–playground complex, Lyle's Los Angelenos and recalling many more all the way back to the safe-spot idea and see-and-be-seen—the activity descriptions make design-related sense only when the interplay between primary actors and significant others is bared. Note, too, that for all the distinctions which scientists make between personal space, privacy, and territoriality, they (as well as the elusive crowding) have one common factor—some inclusionary or exclusionary interaction between subjects.

Dynamite! What Brolin and Zeisel have dealt us is an indicator, a single factor which, upon revelation, will most likely encompass all the components of the sociopsychological agenda in force. Searches for indicators are familiar quests in site design where judgments must be made about the impact of human use upon sets of interlocking variables. Such indicator hunting is most notable among natural-resource factors where now designers must one by one weigh soils, slopes, vegetation, surface and subsurface water patterns, animal habitats, climate, etc. Many studies have been put to isolating a single factor, say soils, asking the question: if we could understand the human intervention outcome upon that factor alone, would it tell us what we need to know about the rest? Thus far, no one factor has been shown to hold that answer in this, an age-old area of design concern. Yet, here we already have our indicator in the newest area of consideration. Could it be that we hesitate in its application because, in this kind of search, we have simply been unaccustomed to success?

Cooper's finding about children playing close to home entries in public housing, the teen gravitation to the pavilion as the first landmark on their way from high school to park, and our discourse on user flows from perimeter enterprises suggest that *convenience* may also enter into the selection of place. Ease of access may also answer why people may be attracted to settings which are less than ideal in lending physical support. Thus, be on the lookout for immediate points of origin just outside as well as within the park.

Utility of the Insights

Physical support: *An analysis of a setting's physical accommodation will tell you something about how best to detail a place for the specific behaviors you have in mind.* Psychological support: *A discernment of a subject's linkage to significant others will tell you much about the advisability of putting up or leaving out barriers and how best to organize use areas in a place.* Convenience: *An understanding of where the users are coming from may tell you something more about where best to locate an activity space.* Thus we have it that behavioral insights gathered through observation may bear significantly upon a place's layout and detailing. That's the heart of design.

Where the site being observed is due for capital improvements, *what-who-where-when-why* information leads to behavioral patterns which deserve to be analyzed as automatically as natural-resource factors in design are now analyzed. Gather the insights casually, if you must. When site rehabilitation is imminent, however, the observations best be documented systematically in order to communicate the findings convincingly to others. Furthermore, in that design work may be commissioned when it is impossible for consultants to manage a good picture of those patterns (say, in the winter or if their offices are far removed from the site), agencies might consider conducting systematic observations ritualistically over peak use times. Call these periodic *behavioral inventories.* In the short range, they may reveal immediate problems to be resolved in house. In the long run, they can serve as an information buildup to be handed to consultants when a major rehabilitation is on line. It is not that one should plan simply on serving existing use.

7.5 What attracts people to particular places?

Throughout, we have been urging only that existing use patterns be given intelligent consideration in planning.

If the observations are to augment the mental encyclopedia and not to improve the site under scrutiny, their utility is in allowing designers eventually to generalize. That mandates that you acquire enough perspective to distinguish between the wholly idiosyncratic and *central tendencies* expected to repeat themselves with similar groups under corresponding conditions. An objection to this I think overblown is that we end up stereotyping people. I grant the necessity to keep up to date. But note that, if you wish to use the word "stereotype," it is not the observer who typecasts the people. He only records what they do. It is the people who stereotype (I prefer "classify") themselves by virtue of tendencies they assume in common with others, and that alone is what joins them under a label.

7.6 Look for central tendencies: who is doing what (where and when), including or excluding whom. Speculate why.

8 Remodeling the Design Process

We now come full circle, back to our opening assertion that a designer predicts behavior by what he does on his plan. The need for behavioral insight has been touted to have particular consequence in people-intensive parks. Indeed, most of our examples have had an urban context where a substantial level of human interaction would be logically expected over most of a site. Behavioral issues may have high-order impact upon decision making in large, resource-oriented recreation places as well—not as much from border to border, perhaps, but certainly in selected areas where people concentrations are just as substantial.

Life tells us that a one-hundred-percent predictability rate is beyond attainment. But that's okay, for we are only after an improved coincidence between what the designer implies will go on and the actual behaviors that take place. Thereby, environmental misfits may diminish in number and surprises may become minimally consequential and spaced far apart. What remains is to change some conditions of design practice that discourage the making of behavioral predictions and thus restrain the productivity of people watching for a purpose in parks.

No Periods, Only Commas

The first inhibitor is the problem-solving process of design itself. Fig. 8.1 shows how it is commonly a linear operation, with a fixed beginning and an absolute end. That end is typically the execution of the construction contract. The designer's usual basis for imagining success is also contained within that frame. Since all he has to go by are his plans and sketches and perhaps a scale model, he limits himself, and not without sense, to items which can be adjudged with a fair amount of accuracy from those media. It's all important stuff: technical matters such as drainage facilitation or material soundness and aesthetic perspectives such as the pleasantness of building approaches. Yet, he is likely to exclude behavioral issues for the simple reason that success or failure in their treatments cannot be determined in the drawing or model stage. Excluded from the measurement end of the process, behavioral factors are susceptible to being glossed over in the decision-making steps as well. It's that old law of priorities at work: the squeaking criterion gets the grease.

Upon occasion, some do appraise a place after the contractor leaves. But mostly the appraisal is for purposes of putting together a magazine promotion or for determining its worthiness for a design award. Curiously, though, we find those same things which it is possible to evaluate in the office forming the basis for the site inspection too. Note this critic's assessment of a fully, constructed place. He dotes exclusively on such familiar themes as: the visual compatibility of buildings and plaza brought about by the "use of matching granite and subtle slanting of vertical planes" and the manner in which the fountain's "geometric pattern of constantly changing columns is relieved by the waywardness of wind and water." It is as if he were looking at no more than perspective sketches or a three-dimensional model. It is opportunity lost, for it leaves untapped the most striking difference between model and reality. The latter has live people, who, coincidentally, are the resource needed for measuring success in treating behavior. The opportunity may be recovered by another way of regarding design routine. See Fig. 8.1 which bends the process all the way around until it's swallowing its tail.

This circular-process model had been in the rhetoric for a while now, urged directly upon designers in recent times by social scientists such as Zeisel, but also smacking of the earlier Gans and Dewey suggestions we discussed for bringing reality into decision making regardless of one's profession. It also mirrors the adage about learning from experience. (Unfortunately, however, the second portion of that ancient adage states that we seldom do.) The circular model extends the job of design past the construction contract as a matter of formality. Thereby,

"LINEAR" DESIGN PROCESS – The Familiar Model

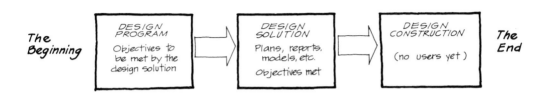

The Beginning

DESIGN PROGRAM

Objectives to be met by the design solution

DESIGN SOLUTION

Plans, reports, models, etc.

Objectives met

DESIGN CONSTRUCTION

(no users yet)

The End

"CIRCULAR" DESIGN PROCESS – An Alternative

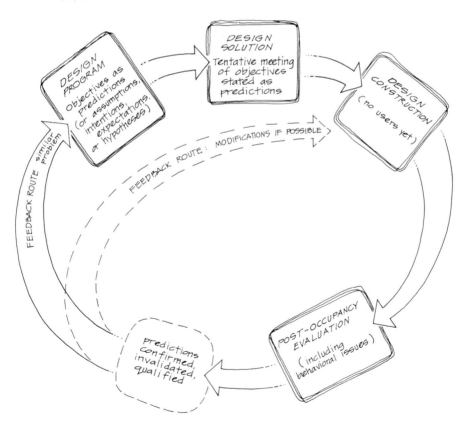

DESIGN PROGRAM

Objectives as Predictions (or assumptions, intentions, expectations, or hypotheses)

DESIGN SOLUTION

Tentative meeting of objectives stated as predictions

DESIGN CONSTRUCTION

(no users yet)

POST-OCCUPANCY EVALUATION

(including behavioral issues)

Predictions confirmed, invalidated, qualified

FEEDBACK ROUTE: similar problem

FEEDBACK ROUTE: MODIFICATIONS IF POSSIBLE

153

this model encourages attention to factors whose tests are found beyond the paper-plan stage. In so doing we may exploit heretofore untapped means for acquiring fresh knowledge and updating old generalizations (or stereotypes, if you still insist).

Before the Fact. To loop the process effectively, two fundamental departures from the linear manner must be made. The first is a subtle amendment in the program phase. The predictions which are usually implied by the plan must be acknowledged out loud. If you're still uncomfortable with the tag "predictions," call them assumptions, intentions, objectives, expectations, or, in the grand old tradition of science, use hypothesis, or, simply, hunch. More important than the term by which the acknowledgment goes, is that it meets the following criteria: *1. It must be measurable.* To say that an aspect of the design will "enrich people's lives" will not do. The pivotal word "enrich" is ambiguous to begin with. Beyond that, how can you really tell? *2. The measurement must be based upon a user response.* The intention of providing a "harmonious composition of textures, colors, and patterns" falls out of order here. A designer need only consult his sensitivity and can answer his question with a great deal of confidence before any users arrive. With those cautions in effect, a good form for the prediction to take would be a paraphrase of architect Michael Brill: "By designing for *these* groups *this* way, I expect X to happen."

This form sets up the tone of inquiry necessary for implementing the idea of design as an experimental process. It begins a roll toward design as a continuum of predictions made, predictions tested, predictions reassessed, new predictions made, or, a process without periods, if you will, only commas.

After the Fact. We must now add a phase for determining the degree to which the predictions prove out, and once more we are confronted by a choice of terms. When it first appeared on the scene, the step for gathering up user reaction was called "Post-Construction Evaluation." Wishing to distinguish it from the magazine and award reviews which typically keyed on how a place was physically put together, it was relabeled "Post-Occupancy Evaluation." The middle-word substitution was to clarify both the timing (not simply following the contractor's clean up, but a bit later on after use) and the investigative focus, i.e., its impact upon those who "occupied" the place. Perhaps thinking that the word evaluation insufficiently implied purpose, Zeisel attached the adjective "diagnostic," which strengthened the idea of searching for cause. Yet if the dictionary definition of diagnosis as "ascertaining the nature and circumstances of a diseased condition" gets read into that, there may follow the instant misbelief that ailment symptoms are assumed to begin with. A Post-Occupancy Evaluation, by any name, makes no a priori presumption of problems present. It is only out to collect evidence in, one might say, the long-run interest of discovering what produces health.

Here, though, we are not engaging in idle word gymnastics. Terminology is important by the way it sets up another tone, one of receptivity by those in a position to use the results of the evaluation. The effectiveness of a Post-Occupancy Evaluation is contingent upon the willingness of the designer to apply the findings. Otherwise, what becomes idle is the phase. This is especially significant when the evaluation is conducted by parties other than those who created the works. They cannot afford the liberties enjoyed by conventional critics whose stake is in appraising something as an end in itself. That is to do no more than to extend the linear process one more step down the road. To keep the roll going in the circular model, the designer's cooperation must be maintained throughout.

Having a mischievous title works against this goal. As I attempted to demonstrate with the possible misreading of diagnosis, there looms the shadow of a faultfinding mission. The constant word evaluation is the biggest troublemaker. It conjures up the similar threat of being "shot down," a phrase whose cold sweat-producing powers is understood well by every former student of design. And you've got to be a masochist to want more of that. That creates a special wariness if the phase is to be addressed routinely to every project (at least theoretically) and not just to the sure things which are usually volunteered for external review.

Because it appears we must live with a troublesome label, other avenues must be worked on to set the cooperative mood. No strategy can be counted on to be entirely successful. Personalities are involved, and a percentage will be untouchable regardless of means. But anything that might alleviate suspicions that the purpose is to throw sand at designers will be a good start. For instance, we should lean away from the emphasis which is championed by many that Post-Occupancy Evaluation is a club for forcing greater accountability for their acts upon designers. It may very well have that result, but I think accountability is better stressed as a side effect. You can't have it both ways: urge experimentation, yet threaten to clobber the guy if it doesn't quite work out. If there be any reference to accountability, it should center on the intelligence put to conceiving the experimental thought. Note from the circular model that the validation component feeds back into the programming phase (or back to the site if physical adjustments are possible). Post-Occupancy Evaluation may thus be seen as a learning tool which gathers up insight in which the requisite intelligence may be founded. In fact, this phase should be stressed less as an evaluation of the project under scrutiny than as a step in programming the next job around.

The manner in which the analysis is conducted may also affect whether the results get used. For the preparation and submission of findings, architect Robert Shibley submits three principles from his studies of organizational conduct:

1. *"Feedback must be descriptive, not evaluative,"* which makes the title of this phase odder yet. That is to say, "Only report what you know, never what you do not know," for if the recipient becomes wounded by extraneous editorializing, the actual facts of the matter may be lost in the equally extraneous defense.
2. *"The presentation of information should not confound what is already a distrustful and threatening environment."* At least don't invoke that condition if it isn't there to begin with. I know. Once I offered post-occupancy findings to designers in a session to which I also invited clients whom I considered well pleased with the designers' work. Despite the usual attempts to balance some negatives with pluses, only the former generated a response, a tight-lipped rebuttal from the designers as they eyed the client busily scribbling notes. To complete everybody's day, I then unveiled a redesign idea prepared by my associates which "improved" the site in light of the findings. The client responded by musing out loud that he had given his people a blank check for executing the job. Enough said. The designers sat contemplating the embarrassment unnecessarily caused them while I edged out of the room wishing only to find a quiet corner to wring out my socks.
3. *"Feedback should be provided only when it is asked for. There is ample evidence in the psychological literature to assert that feedback is only useful when desired."* Working against this principle are evaluations which are conducted as fishing expeditions or simply attend to the researcher's bias (e.g., he's an expert in territorial behavior, so he limits his analysis to what bears upon that). I have already hinted my preference for a third route which keys the inspection to the designer's expressed intentions. This route heightens the cast of service to the designer (and, if he is in on it from the beginning, the client), for it strikes at what he might be most interested in knowing. Therefore, the prospects that the feedback will be used are advanced.

Regardless, some initial focus such as designer's intentions seems necessary because there is not yet a universal framework for conducting a post occupancy test. A full-bore systematic investigation usually calls out many evidence-collecting devices, from interview and questionnaire instruments through observation-recording tools, which may range from notebook formats to video and time-lapse movie cameras. In the sense that it is the question(s) being asked, the focus suggests the kind of evidence needed and, as such, directs both the selection of instruments and the specifics of their design.

Considering the absence of uniform procedure, the best introduction to anything approaching a "complete" methodology will be found in the most sophisticated case study you can get your hands on. Appendix B shows some of the steps which could be involved. With only a cursory glance, you may rightly infer that an in-depth investigation will be labor-intensive and time-consuming, neither of which a typical design office may be able to afford. Nor may design practitioners have the skills on line to execute effectively all aspects of the task. More than likely, a special team of consultants will be needed, and, indeed, a few outfits geared to that service have begun to spring up. That brings us a crucial question. Not only has a step been added to the design process, but quite probably another layer of bodies as well. Who pays for the work? A goodly number of evaluations thus far accomplished have been by university professors and their students as an extension of classroom activity and have been therefore pretty much on the cheap side. For the most part, the funding for investigations conducted by professional consultants has come from widely spaced government grants. Although it may rub contrary to some political religions, I suspect any financing breakthroughs of major scale will evolve from governmental sources, too. In that it might become more and more apparent that construction dollars and user aggravations (read, votes) would be saved in subsequent go-rounds through applications of post-occupancy feedback, we may even get legislation requiring the phase for at least public contracts. The case here is strengthened with the perception of Post-Occupancy Evaluation as a programming strategy. That would make the move consistent with legislation presently on the books which mandates public input in conventional programming. The programming angle may tempt the private sector as well.

Let's separate the issues. Funding obstacles notwithstanding, the merits of post-occupancy feedback remain, and many small steps can still be taken within the framework of standard office routine to close the loop. Casual observations can accomplish much. But the productivity of even this simplest means also hinges on the forthright phrasing of the plan predictions. That forms the questions that start the circular model in motion; from there, it is a matter of picking your time to look. Still too demanding? Then try this: *Choose from your list of predictions the* one *whose outcome most interests you,* and simply attend to that. More painless yet for park designers, they can take their families along for an enjoyable outing. Yet because their eyes are open on business, they can write off the trip.

157

A staff habit of isolating number-one predictions can also sharpen office conversations as curiosities become developed over why the selection was made. Indeed, such sharing can add a new dimension to the weekly wine-and-cheese, "keeping current" seminars that many firms encourage their employees to conduct.

Let's Hear It for the Good Guys

A second inhibitor of the widespread consideration of behavioral factors is the reward system which the design professions have arranged among themselves. Note the decided "thing" orientation in the criteria for design awards, competitions, and professional society prizes or, similarly, in the judgment commentary if the criteria are not predetermined. Indeed, look at the photos of the prizewinners submitted to impress the juries. Even though there may be great variations in project types, most have a striking absence of people. It is as if a mess of people will get in the way of the places' visual or technical wonders. And, of course, that's what will decide which design takes the cup.

A way back, we mentioned that the prospect of an immediate and tangible gain is a powerful force behind effecting behavioral change. As a means for admitting the behavioral dimension into routine practice, the design award holds that promise. Consider then amending the competition system, at least for the major prizes whose prestige may be sufficient to compensate for the extra hassle involved. Begin by requiring that submissions undergo a shakedown period of use. Two years seems just about right. Then add to the usual technical and aesthetic criteria a request for evidence on how behavioral assumptions worked out. One version would have all entries adjudged by conventional measures and the usual honor awards handed out. All of the honored designs in each category would then be evaluated for behavioral congruence within the following year and those which proved superior presented a supernumary citation at the next big presentation bash as last year's "best of show."

Who performs the post-occupancy test? Pardon the indulgence, but university professors and their students should not be overlooked as a resource. The nature of the task is well suited to the exercise level and therefore can yield telling results without posing competition for consultants who are necessarily attracted to more extensive assignments to make their living. Even pare down the inquiry to the designer's choice of that one prediction that interested him the most. That may be a bit too self-serving for a contest, yet it may work well as a trial piece to start the behavioral dimension on its way to visibility.

I know of only one formal instance where an award incentive was offered for behaviorally based criteria in the design of parks. You have to look hard for it! Down at the bottom of the sample judging form for an annual West Coast statewide competition, I discovered the question: "Does the park function as intended?" Except to mention that it would be helpful to submit a few photos showing people, the form does not indicate how that might be demonstrated. And it's worth only five points more than filling out the entry blank correctly. Nevertheless, here we have from practice a formal acknowledgment of what these pages have suggested is good. I like to think of it as a harbinger of things to come.

Footnote

I have not named any of the sites which have provided my examples in order to direct attention away from any one place as a subject of query to the lessons gained from looking at many. The absence of site names is also to reinforce the idea put forth under Post-Occupancy Evaluation but applicable to the people-watching process per se: it is less to evaluate the project under scrutiny than a step in programming the next job around. My references to geographical locations are included to show that insightful demonstrations are all around us, wherever we happen to be. My occasional lapsing into family experiences is included to indicate that useful examples can be as close as that.

All of the sketches represent real instances, either copied directly from slides or from verbal descriptions of events that have been witnessed without benefit of camera in hand. I have opted for sketches only, instead of a mélange of prints from my slides and drawings to fill in the blanks. I thought it best to go for a uniform appearance. After all, one cannot be expected to put aside every aspect of professional acculturation.

The examples, though, have not been put forth to "prove" anything, only to suggest potential payoffs as enticements for generating the best kind of proof—what you know from your own experience. Thus if you were to succumb to only one urging found on these pages, may it be that you go out forthwith . . . and see for yourself.

161

Appendix A

A Debriefing Instrument for Behavioral Observations

To help seat observational insights in your mind, you may wish to jot down highlights on this form after having witnessed a significant episode. Accordingly, type up a master similar to this exhibit, leaving enough room between each item for notations. Reproduce a good number of them and keep them handy. This form may also be adapted for use as a field instrument for conducting systematic observations.

If you want to keep a running account of your observations, place a batch of forms in a looseleaf notebook with a blank sheet separating each set. (Consider using colored stock for the blank sheet to make the separations obvious.) When the notebook is opened, the first typed sheet should appear to the right with the blank on the left. The blank face can then be used to rough out a plan of the place upon which you can also dot in the location of the subjects in the fashion of a density diagram. Use the blank backs of subsequent notation pages for additional sketches if desired. To each set, you may also add a plastic sheet commercially available with pockets for the insertion of slides. Key each slide back to the relevant notation.

Observation Record

Data

Place _____ Weather _____

Day/Date/Time _____ _____

What: Specify behaviors observed. People present or traces?

Who: Cultural heritage, social class, life-cycle stage, role, sex as relevant.

Where: Plot on adjacent map. Describe more exactly here.

Diagnosis

Why: Physical attributes of the setting.

Relationship of primary actors to significant others.

Observation Record

Did the users adapt the setting; adapt to the setting? How so?

How does the design's layout and/or detailing hinder for facilitate the behaviors?

Is the place being used according to the designer's interactions?

Are the environmental cues attracting or discouraging the behaviors?

Observation Record

Grist for Generalizing

Are there tendencies reminiscent of something you have observed before?

Does the episode exemplify a particular behavioral theory?

Anything unique about the who (and when) that generated the what in the specific where?

Anything else as a carryover for dealing with a design of a similar kind?

Appendix B

A Post-occupancy Evaluation Procedure Model

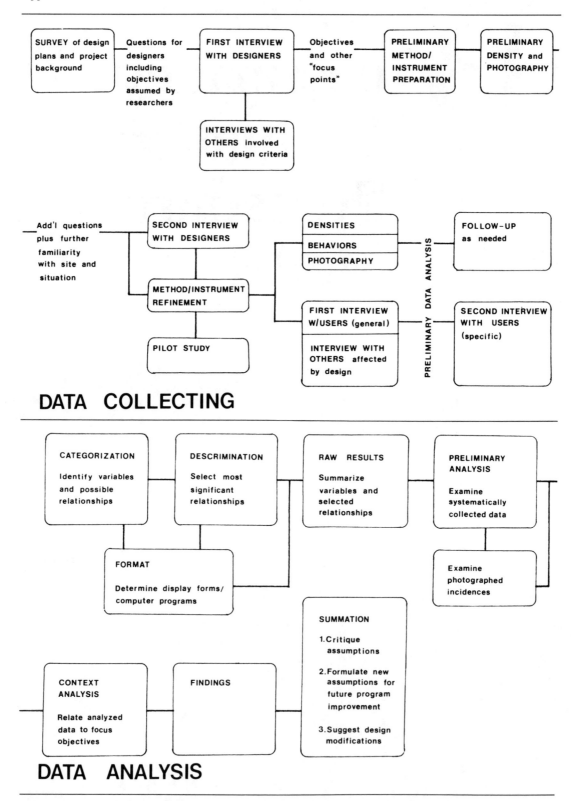

SURVEY of design plans and project background

Questions for designers including objectives assumed by researchers

FIRST INTERVIEW WITH DESIGNERS

Objectives and other "focus points"

PRELIMINARY METHOD/ INSTRUMENT PREPARATION

PRELIMINARY DENSITY and PHOTOGRAPHY

INTERVIEWS WITH OTHERS involved with design criteria

Add'l questions plus further familiarity with site and situation

SECOND INTERVIEW WITH DESIGNERS

DENSITIES
BEHAVIORS
PHOTOGRAPHY

FOLLOW-UP as needed

METHOD/INSTRUMENT REFINEMENT

FIRST INTERVIEW W/USERS (general)

SECOND INTERVIEW WITH USERS (specific)

INTERVIEW WITH OTHERS affected by design

PILOT STUDY

PRELIMINARY DATA ANALYSIS

DATA COLLECTING

CATEGORIZATION

Identify variables and possible relationships

DESCRIMINATION

Select most significant relationships

RAW RESULTS

Summarize variables and selected relationships

PRELIMINARY ANALYSIS

Examine systematically collected data

FORMAT

Determine display forms/ computer programs

Examine photographed incidences

SUMMATION

1. Critique assumptions

2. Formulate new assumptions for future program improvement

3. Suggest design modifications

CONTEXT ANALYSIS

Relate analyzed data to focus objectives

FINDINGS

DATA ANALYSIS

Bibliography

Alexander, Christopher, Sara Ishikawa, Murray Silverstein, with Max
　　Jacobson, Ingrid Fiksdahl-King, and Shlomo Angel: *A Pattern
　　Language: Towns, Buildings, Construction,* Oxford University Press,
　　New York, 1977.

———, ———, Sanford Hirshen, Shlomo Angel, and Christie Coffin:
　　Houses Generated by Patterns, Center for Environmental Structure,
　　Berkeley, Calif. 1969.

Allen, Patricia R. B., and Albert J. Rutledge: *An Annotated Bibliography
　　of Mostly Obscure Articles on Human Territorial Behavior,* Council of
　　Planning Librarians, Monticello, Ill., March 1975.

———, Cherie Kluesing, and Laurie MacMillan: *An Annotated Bibliography
　　on Play Environments: Planning, Design and Evaluation,* Department of
　　Landscape Architecture, University of Illinois, Urbana-Cham-
　　paign, 1976.

Altman, Irwin: *Environment and Social Behavior: Privacy, Personal Space, Terri-
　　tory and Crowding,* Brooks/Cole, Monterey, Calif., 1975.

———, and Joachim F. Wohlwill: *Human Behavior and Environment: Ad-
　　vances in Theory and Research, Vol. 1,* Plenum Press, New York, 1976.

———: *Human Behavior and Environment: Advances in Theory and Research,
　　Vol. 2,* Plenum Press, New York, 1977.

———: *Human Behavior and Environment: Advances in Theory and Research:
　　Children and the Environment, Vol. 3,* Plenum Press, New York, 1978.

Ardrey, Robert: *The Hunting Hypothesis: A Personal Conclusion Concerning
　　the Evolutionary Nature of Man,* Atheneum, New York, 1976.

———: *The Territorial Imperative: A Personal Inquiry into the Animal Origins
　　of Property and Nations,* Atheneum, New York, 1966.

Barker, Roger G.: *Ecological Psychology: Concepts and Methods for Studying
　　the Environment of Human Behavior,* Stanford University Press, Stan-
　　ford, Calif., 1968.

———(ed.): *The Stream of Behavior: Explorations of Its Structure and Content,*
　　Appleton-Century-Crofts, New York, 1963.

Bechtel, Robert B.: *Enclosing Behavior,* Dowden, Hutchinson & Ross,
　　Stroudsburg, Penn., 1977.

Becker, Franklin D.: "A Class-Conscious Evaluation: Going Back to
　　Sacramento's Pedestrian Mall," *Landscape Architecture,* vol. 64, 1973,
　　pp. 448–457.

———: *Design for Living: The Resident's View of Multi-Family Housing,* Center
　　for Urban Development Research, Cornell University, Ithaca,
　　N.Y., 1974.

———: "Evaluating the Sacramento Mall," *Design & Environment,* vol. 2,
　　no. 4, Winter 1971, p. 38.

Bengtsson, Arvid: *Adventure Playgrounds,* Praeger, New York, 1972.

———: *Environmental Planning for Children's Play*, Praeger, New York, 1970.

Berelson, Bernard, and Gary A. Steiner: *Human Behavior: An Inventory of Scientific Findings*, Harcourt Brace Jovanovich, New York, 1964.

Berg, Lynn: *Crime Prevention Review for Fridley Neighborhood Parks*, Minnesota Crime Prevention Center, Minneapolis, 1979.

Birdwhistell, Ray: *Introduction to Kinesics*, University of Louisville, Louisville, 1952.

Braybrooke, Susan: "Evaluating Evaluation," *Design and Environment*, vol. 5, no. 3, Fall 1974a, pp. 20–25.

———: "Watching a People Watcher," *Design and Environment*, 3vol. 5, no. 3, Fall, 1974b, pp. 26–29.

Broady, Maurice: *Planning for People*, Bedford Square Press of The National Council of Social Service, London, 1968.

Brolin, Brent C.: *The Failure of Modern Architecture*, Van Nostrand Reinhold, New York, 1976.

———: "The Risks in Designing for Other Cultures," *Landscape Architecture*, November 1977, p. 521.

———, and John Zeisel: "Mass Housing: Social Research and Design," *Architectural Forum*, July/August 1968, pp. 66–71.

Byerts, Thomas O., and Joseph D. Teaff: "Social Research as a Design Tool," *Parks & Recreation*, vol. 10, no. 1, 1975, pp. 34–36, 62–66.

Callecod, Robert L.: "Play Preferences of Selected Grade School Children on Varying Types of Playground Equipment," master's thesis, University of Illinois, Urbana-Champaign, 1974.

Canter, David: *The Psychology of Place*, The Architectural Press, London, 1977.

Chapin, F. Stuart: *Human Activity Patterns in the City: Things People Do in Time and in Space*, Wiley, New York, 1974.

Chermayeff, Serge, and Christopher Alexander: *Community and Privacy: Towards a New Architecture of Humanism*, Anchor Books, Garden City, New York, 1963.

Clay, Grady: "What Makes a Good Square Good?," *Landscape Architecture*, November 1978, pp. 483–484.

Conway, Donald J. (ed.): *Human Response to Tall Buildings*, Dowden, Hutchinson & Ross, Stroudsburg, Penn., 1977.

Cook, Robert S., Jr.: "Watching Where You Sit . . . and Stand," *Urban Land*, October 1977, pp. 11–16.

Cooper, Clare C.: *Easter Hill Village: Some Special Implications of Design*, The Free Press, New York, 1975.

———: *Resident Attitudes Towards the Development at St. Francis Square, San Francisco: A Summary of the Initial Findings*, Institute of Urban and Regional Development, Work Paper No. 126, University of California, Berkeley, 1972.

———: "St. Francis Square: Attitudes of Its Residents," *American Institute of Architects Journal*, December 1971, pp. 22–27.

———, and Phyllis Hackett: *Analysis of the Design Process at Two Moderate-Income Housing Developments*, Institute of Urban and Regional Studies, University of California, Berkeley, 1968.

Cooper-Hewitt Museum: *Urban Open Spaces*, The Museum, New York, 1979.

Dattner, Richard: *Design for Play*, Van Nostrand Reinhold, New York, 1969.

Dean, Andrea O.: "Evaluation: A Much-Praised Housing Project Nearly

Becomes 'The West Coast's Pruitt-Igoe," *American Institute of Architects Journal*, August 1976, pp. 22–25.

Dean, Larry M., William M. Pugh, and E. K. Eric Gunderson: "The Behavioral Effect of Crowding: Definitions and Methods," *Environment and Behavior*, vol. 10, no. 3, September 1978, pp. 419–433.

Deasy, C. M.: *Design for Human Affairs*, Wiley, New York, 1974.

————: "People-Watching with a Purpose," *American Institute of Architects Journal*, Vol. 54, no. 6, December 1970, pp. 35–40.

DeJonge, D.: "Applied Hodology," *Landscape*, vol. 17, no. 2, 1967, pp. 10–11.

Dubos, René: *Man Adapting*, Yale University Press, New Haven, Conn., 1965.

————: "Man Overadapting," *Psychology Today*, February 1971, pp. 50–53.

————: *So Human an Animal*, Scribner, New York, 1968.

Ellis, M. J.: *Play: Theory and Research*, Motor Performance and Play Research Laboratory, Children's Research Center, University of Illinois, Urbana-Champaign, 1971.

Esser, Aristide H., and Barrie B. Greenbie: *Design for Communality and Privacy*, Plenum Press, New York, 1978.

Farbstein, Jay: *People in Places: Experiencing, Using and Changing the Built Environment*, Prentice-Hall, Englewood Cliffs, N.J., 1978.

Fast, Julius: *Body Language*, Pocket Books, New York, 1970.

Francescato, Guido, Sue Weidemann, James R. Anderson, and Richard Chenoweth: *Residents' Satisfaction in HUD-Assisted Housing: Design and Management Factors*, Report to the U.S. Department of Housing and Urban Development by the University of Illinois Housing Research and Development Program, Government Printing Office, Washington, D.C., 1979.

Freedman, Jonathan L.: *Crowding and Behavior*, Viking Press, New York, 1975.

Friedberg, Paul M.: *Play and Interplay*, Macmillan, New York, 1970.

Friedmann, Arnold, Craig Zimring, and Ervin Zube: *Environmental Design Evaluation*, Plenum Press, New York, 1978.

Gans, Herbert J.: *The Levittowners*, Pantheon Books, New York, 1967.

————: *People and Plans: Essays on Urban Problems and Solutions*, Basic Books, New York, 1968.

————: *The Urban Villagers*, The Free Press, New York, 1962.

Gardiner, Richard A.: "Crime and the Neighborhood Environment," *HUD Challenge*, February 1976, pp. 9–13.

Goffman, Erving: *Behavior in Public Places: Notes on the Social Organization of Gatherings*, Free Press, New York, 1963.

————: *Strategic Interaction*, University of Pennsylvania Press, Philadelphia, 1969.

Gold, Seymour M.: "Deviant Behavior in Urban Parks," *Journal of Health, Physical Education, and Recreation*, November/December 1974, pp. 50–52.

————: "Nonuse of Neighborhood Parks," *American Institute of Planners Journal*, November 1972, pp. 369–378.

Greenbie, Barrie B.: "Social Territory, Community Health and Urban Planning," *American Institute of Planners Journal*, March 1974, pp. 74–82.

Gump, Paul: "The Behavior Setting," *Landscape Architecture*, January 1971, pp. 130–135.

Gutman, Robert (ed.): *People and Buildings*, Basic Books, New York, 1972.
———: "Site Planning and Social Behavior," *Journal of Social Issues*, vol. 22, no. 4, October 1966, pp. 103–115.
Hall, Edward T.: *Beyond Culture*, Anchor Press, Garden City, N.Y., 1976.
———: *The Hidden Dimension*, Doubleday, New York, 1966.
———: *The Silent Language*, Doubleday, New York, 1959.
Halprin, Lawrence: *New York, New York: A Study of the Quality, Character and Meaning of Open Space in Urban Design*, Report to the Housing and Development Administration, City of New York, 1968.
———: *The RSVP Cycles: Creative Processes in the Human Environment*, Braziller, New York, 1969.
Heckscher, August, with Phyllis Robinson: *Open Spaces: The Life of American Cities*, Harper & Row, New York, 1977.
Heimsath, Clovis: *Behavioral Architecture: Toward an Accountable Design Process*, McGraw-Hill, New York, 1977.
Hester, Randolph T.: *Neighborhood Space*, Dowden, Hutchinson & Ross, Stroudsburg, Penn., 1975.
———: "A Womb With a View: How Spatial Nostalgia Affects the Designer," *Landscape Architecture*, September 1979, pp. 475–481.
Holahan, Charles J.: *Environment and Behavior: A Dynamic Perspective*, Plenum Press, New York, 1979.
Insel, Paul M., and Henry Clay Lindgren: *Too Close for Comfort: The Psychology of Crowding*, Prentice-Hall, Englewood Cliffs, N.J., 1978.
Jackson, Edward, David B. Pinson, Janice Ward, and Arthur Flaks: *Bibliography on Vandalism*, Vance Bibliographies, Monticello, Ill., September 1978.
Jackson, J. B.: "Notes and Comments," *Landscape*, Winter 1967–1968, pp. 1–3.
Jacobs, Jane: *The Death and Life of Great American Cities*, Random House, New York, 1961.
Joardar, S. D., and J. W. Neill: "The Subtle Differences in Configuration of Vancouver's Small Public Spaces," *Landscape Architecture*, November 1978, pp. 487–491.
Joyner, Louis: "The Changing Playscape," *Southern Living*, September 1976, pp. 51–55.
Johnson, Bruce A.: *Recommendations Regarding the Application of the Behavior Setting Unit in the Environmental Design Process*, master's thesis, University of Illinois, Urbana-Champaign, 1971.
Kaplan, Stephan, and Rachel Kaplan: *Humanscape: Environments for People*, Duxbury Press, Belmont, Calif., 1978.
Kato, Hidetoshi (ed.), with William H. Whyte, Randolph David, Margaret Bemiss, and Rebecca Erwin: *A Comparative Study of Street Life: Tokyo, Manila, New York*, Occasional Papers, no. 5, Research Institute for Oriental Cultures, Gakushuin University, Tokyo, 1978.
Keller, Suzanne: *The Urban Neighborhood: A Sociological Perspective*, Random House, New York, 1968.
Kira, Alexander: *The Bathroom: Criteria for Design*, Bantam Books, New York, 1966.
Krog, Steven R.: "Columbus, Indiana: A Mecca Minus Landscape," *Landscape Architecture*, January 1977, pp. 62–68.
———: "Evaluation: The Fabric of Roosevelt Island: A Look at New York's Experimental New Town from a Site Planning Viewpoint," *American Institute of Architects Journal*, May 1979, pp. 38–47.

Lang, Jon, Charles Burnette, Walter Moleski, and David Vachon: *Designing for Human Behavior: Architecture and the Behavioral Sciences*, Dowden, Hutchinson & Ross, Stroudsburg, Penn., 1974.

Laurie, Ian C.: "Over-Design Is the Death of Outdoor Liveliness," *Landscape Architecture*, November 1978, pp. 485–486.

Leighton, Alexander H.: *My Name Is Legion: Foundations for a Theory of Man in Relation to Culture, Vol. I, The Stirling County Study of Psychiatric Disorder and Sociocultural Environment*, Basic Books, New York, 1959.

Lerup, Lars: "Environmental and Behavioral Congruence as a Measure of Goodness in Public Space: The Case of Stockholm," *Ekistics*, no. 204, November 1972, pp. 341–358.

Linday, Nancy: "Drawing Socio-Economic Lines in Central Park," *Landscape Architecture*, November 1977, pp. 515–520.

———: "It All Comes Down to a Comfortable Place to Sit and Watch in San Francisco," *Landscape Architecture*, November 1978, pp. 492–496.

Lyle, J. T.: "People Watching in Parks," *Landscape Architecture*, vol. 61, no. 1, 1970, pp. 31, 51–52.

Mackie, Robert: "Viewpoint: Chuckholes in the Bumpy Road from Research to Application," *Behavior Today*, vol. 5, no. 41, November 1974, pp. 295–296.

Maslow, Abraham: *Motivation and Personality*, Harper & Row, New York, 1954.

Mehrabian, Albert: *Public Places and Private Spaces: The Psychology of Work, Play, and Living Environments*, Basic Books, New York, 1976.

———, and James A. Russell: *An Approach to Environmental Psychology*, M.I.T. Press, Cambridge, Mass., 1974.

Michelson, William: *Behavioral Research Methods in Environmental Design*, Dowden, Hutchinson & Ross, Stroudsburg, Penn., 1975.

———: *Environmental Choice, Human Behavior and Residential Satisfaction*, Oxford University Press, London, 1977.

———: *Man and His Urban Environment: A Sociological Approach*, First Edition, Second Edition, Addison-Wesley, Reading, Mass., 1970, 1976.

———: "Most People Don't Want What Architects Want," *TransAction*, July/August 1968, pp. 37–43.

Moore, Gary T., and Reginald G. Golledge (eds.): *Environmental Knowing: Theories, Research and Methods*, Dowden, Hutchinson & Ross, Stroudsburg, Penn., 1976.

Moos, Rudolph H., and Paul M. Insel (eds.): *Issues in Social Ecology*, National Press Books, Palo Alto, Calif., 1974.

Morris, Desmond: *Manwatching: A Field Guide to Human Behavior*, Abrams, New York, 1977.

Myhrum, David R.: *The Street as a Human Resource in the Urban Lower-Class Environment*, master's thesis, University of Illinois, Urbana-Champaign, 1972.

Newman, Oscar: *Defensible Space: Crime Prevention Through Urban Design*, Macmillan, New York, 1972.

New York City Planning Commission: *New Life for Plazas*, The Commission, New York, 1975.

Pablant, Pavel, and James C. Baxter: "Environmental Correlates of School Vandalism," *American Institute of Planners Journal*, July 1975, pp. 270–279.

Parr, A. E.: "Environmental Design and Psychology," *Landscape*, Winter 1964–1965, pp. 15–18.

Pastalan, Leon A., and Daniel H. Carson (ed.): *Spatial Behavior of Older People*, The University of Michigan-Wayne State University Institute of Gerontology, Ann Arbor, 1970.

Perin, Constance: *Everything in Its Place: Social Order and Land Use in America*, Princeton University Press, Princeton, N.J., 1977.

Peterson, Peggy: "The Id and the Image: Human Needs and Design Implications," *Landmark*, 1966, pp. 8–15.

Piaget, Jean, and Barbel Inhelder: *The Psychology of the Child*, Basic Books, New York, 1969.

Pinfold, Zara: *An Analysis of Family Life Cycle Phase Groups as a Basis for Generating Planning and Design Goals for Outdoor Neighborhood Leisure*, master's thesis, University of Illinois, Urbana-Champaign, 1979.

Porteous, J. Douglas: *Environment and Behavior: Planning and Everyday Urban Life*, Addison-Wesley, Reading Mass., 1977.

Preiser, Wolfgang F. E. (ed.): *Facility Programming: Methods and Applications*, Dowden, Hutchinson & Ross, Stroudsburg, Penn., 1978.

Project for Public Spaces, Inc.: *Chase Manhattan Plaza Study*, The Project New York, 1975.

——: *Euclid Avenue: A Street for People*, The Project New York, 1978.

——: *Exxon Minipark*, The Project New York, 1978.

——: *Gateway National Recreation Area: Riis Park Study*, The Project New York, 1977.

——: *Greenacre Park*, The Project, New York, 1977.

——: *125th Street Study*, The Project, New York, 1976.

——: *Planning and Zoning for Public Spaces in Seattle*, The Project, New York, 1977.

——: *Plazas for People*, The Project, New York, 1978.

——: *Plazas for People: Seattle Federal Building Plaza Case Study*, The Project, New York, 1977.

——: *Plazas for People: Seattle First National Bank Plaza*, The Project, New York, 1977.

——: *Public Space Evaluation: Pennsylvania Avenue and the Federal Triangle*, The Project, New York, 1978.

——: *Rockefeller Center: Concourse Signage Study*, The Project, New York, 1976.

——: *West 46th Street: A Plan for Improvement*, The Project, New York, 1978.

Proshansky, Harold M., William H. Ittleson, and Leanne G. Rivlin (eds.): *Environmental Psychology*, First Edition, Second Edition, Holt, Rinehart & Winston, New York, 1970, 1976.

Rainwater, Lee: *Behind Ghetto Walls*, Aldine, Chicago, 1970.

Rand, Ayn: *The Fountainhead*, Bobbs-Merrill, Indianapolis, 1943.

Rapoport, Amos: *House Form and Culture*, Prentice-Hall, Englewood Cliffs, N.J., 1969.

——: *Human Aspects of Urban Form: Towards a Man-Environment Approach to Urban Form and Design*, First Edition, Pergamon Press, New York, 1977.

—— (ed.): *The Mutual Interaction of People and Their Built Environment: A Cross-Cultural Perspective*, Aldine, Illinois, 1976.

Rapoport, Rhona, and Robert N. Rapoport, with the collaboration of Ziona Strelitz: *Leisure and the Family Life Cycle*, Routledge & Kegan Paul, London, 1975.

Rudolph, Nancy: *Workyards: Playgrounds Planned for Adventure*, Teachers College Press, Columbia University, New York, 1974.

Reusch, Jurgen, and Weldon Kees: *Nonverbal Communication: Notes on the Visual Perception of Human Relations*, University of California Press, Berkeley, 1956.

Rutledge, Albert J.: *Anatomy of a Park*, McGraw-Hill, New York, 1971.

———: *First National Bank Plaza, Chicago, Illinois: A Pilot Study in Post Construction Evaluation*, Department of Landscape Architecture, University of Illinois, Urbana-Champaign, 1975.

———: "Looking Beyond the Applause at Chicago's First National Bank Plaza," *Landscape Architecture*, January 1976, pp. 55–59.

———: "Playground Design with a Motive in Mind," *Parks & Recreation*, vol. 10, no. 2, 1975, pp. 20–22, 43–44.

Saarinen, Thomas F.: *Environmental Planning: Perception and Behavior*, Houghton Mifflin, Boston, 1976.

Schmidt, Donald E., Roy D. Goldman, and Nickolaus R. Feimer: "Perceptions of Crowding: Predicting at the Residence, Neighborhood, and City Levels," *Environment and Behavior*, vol. 11, no. 1, March 1979, pp. 105–131.

Sheehy, Gail: *Passages: Predictable Crisis of Adult Life*, Bantam Books, New York, 1976.

Sommer, Robert: *Design Awareness*, Rinehart Press, San Francisco, 1972.

———: *Personal Space: The Behavioral Basis of Design*, Prentice-Hall, Englewood Cliffs, N.J., 1969.

———: *Tight Spaces: Hard Architecture and How to Humanize It*, Prentice-Hall, Englewood Cliffs, N.J., 1974.

———, and Franklin D. Becker: "The Old Men in Plaza Park," *Landscape Architecture*, vol. 60, no. 1, January 1969, pp. 111–114.

———, and Robert L. Thayer, Jr.: "The Radicalization of Common Ground: People's Park, Berkeley," *Landscape Architecture*, November 1977, pp. 510–514.

Stephens, Suzanne (moderator): "Design as a Tool for Social Change," *Design & Environment*, vol. 3, no. 2, 1972, pp. 43–45.

Stewart, J., and Ricki L. McKenzie: "Composing Urban Spaces for Security, Privacy and Outlook," *Landscape Architecture*, September 1978, pp. 392–398.

Stone, Susan C., and John W. Taylor: *Inner City Turnaround: An Evolving Plan for a Total Service Neighborhood, Longview-Torrence Park, Decatur, Illinois*, Housing Research and Development Program, University of Illinois, Urbana-Champaign, 1976.

Studer, Raymond G., and David Stea: "Architectural Programming, Environmental Design, and Human Behavior," *Journal of Social Issues*, vol. 22, no. 4, 1966, pp. 127–136.

Suttles, Gerald D.: *The Social Order of the Slum*, University of Chicago Press, Chicago, 1968.

Taylor, Bill: "Cruising, Porch-Sitting, Cycling—Designs Fit Neighborhood Patterns in Decatur, Illinois," *Landscape Architecture*, September 1978, pp. 399–404.

Thomsen, Charles E.: "Open Spaces: Their Shape and Scale," *American Institute of Architects Journal*, December 1970, pp. 30–34.

Toffler, Alvin: *Future Shock*, Random House, New York, 1970.

Tuan, Yi-Fu: "Raw Emotion to Intellectual Delight—Landscape's Affective Domain," *Landscape Architecture*, March 1978, pp. 132–134.

———: *Space and Place: The Perspective of Experience*, University of Minnesota Press, Minneapolis, 1977.

Tuan, Yi-fu: *Topophilia: A Study of Environmental Perception, Attitudes and Values*, Prentice-Hall, Englewood Cliffs, N.J., 1974.

Van der Ryn, Sim, and Murray Silverstein: *Dorms at Berkeley: An Environmental Analysis*, Center for Planning and Development Research, Berkeley, Calif., 1967.

Ward, Colin: *The Child in the City*, Pantheon Books, New York, 1978.

———(ed.): *Vandalism*, Van Nostrand Reinhold, New York, 1973.

Webb, Eugene J., Donald T. Campbell, Richard D. Schwartz, and Lee Sechrest: *Unobtrusive Measures: Nonreactive Research in the Social Sciences*, Rand McNally, Chicago, Illinois, 1966.

Whyte, William H.: "The Best Street Life in the World: Why Schmoozing, Smooching, Noshing, Ogling Are Getting Better All the Time," *New York*, vol. 7, no. 28, July 1974, pp. 26–33.

———: "Please, Just a Nice Place to Sit," *New York Times Sunday Magazine*, December 3, 1972, pp. 20 ff.

———: *The Social Life of Small Urban Spaces*, The Conservation Foundation, Washington, D.C., 1980.

Zeisel, John: *Schoolhouse*, Educational Facilities Laboratories Newsletter, no. 15, New York, March 1974.

———: *Social Science Frontiers: Sociology and Architectural Design*, Russell Sage, New York, 1975.

———, and Mary Griffin: *Charlesview Housing: A Diagnostic Evaluation*, Architecture Research Office Graduate School of Design, Cambridge, Mass., 1975.

Index